John Douglas S. Argyll

From Shadow to Sunlight

John Douglas S. Argyll

From Shadow to Sunlight

ISBN/EAN: 9783744743839

Printed in Europe, USA, Canada, Australia, Japan

Cover: Foto ©Thomas Meinert / pixelio.de

More available books at **www.hansebooks.com**

From Shadow to Sunlight

BY THE
MARQUIS OF LORNE, G.C.M.G.

AUTHOR OF

LOVE AND PERIL, A STORY OF THE FAR NORTHWEST, ETC.

NEW YORK
D. APPLETON AND COMPANY
1891

Authorized Edition.

FROM SHADOW TO SUNLIGHT.

CHAPTER I.

"Oh, let me see the cavern. Do take me if the weather be fine enough," said a beautiful American girl, who with her father was visiting Europe, and had found her way to a Scotch country house, after tasting of the joys of the London season. Her father was a gentleman who had been in office in New York State, but had given up public life for the leisure which he loved to use for travel and reading. As in the case of most Americans who love literature, he had at his fingers' ends most of our great authors. Scott's novels had of course made him wish to see Scotland, and he had gladly accepted for himself and daughter an invitation given to him by the proprietor of some wild coast and moorland on the West of Ross.

"Well," he said, after his daughter had spoken, "I am of Dr. Johnson's opinion in the matter of caves. There is hardly one that repays the trouble of a scramble down into their gloomy passages. Even in the Kentucky Mammoth Cave or those of Virginia I have been very glad to escape from the underground corridors and holes, although they are filled with exquisite and elegant stalactitic forms, and to leave them all behind, again to emerge and breathe the free air of heaven."

"Yes, sir, you are right with dear old Sam Johnson," said the old laird who venerated the great Sam, his dictionary and everything that he had ever written, with the reverence often shown by a simple-minded gentleman for a literary bear; "but Sam Johnson himself was much pleased with a cave on a neighboring coast not unlike that one which I desire

to show to you to-day. You will here experience none of the unpleasant sensa-
tions of being in a hole underground, for
you will be able to see the ocean from a
great part of the interior, and light coming from the sea even in its largest hall,
though not beyond that."

"If you and my daughter unite your
forces, I yield with the best grace," and
so the matter was settled to the young
lady's great delight. She had much enjoyed her "good time" in England, and
was prepared to be as enthusiastic about
Highland scenery as she had been about
Westminster Abbey. She liked the freedom of life in the country house, where
two or three of the bachelors were already
devoted to her, and willing even to forego
a day's grouse shooting or stalking to
take part in any expedition she might in-
dicate as agreeable to her somewhat way-
ward fancy. She had charmed the old
laird by insisting on playing chess of an

evening with him. He was a venerable
ancient who looked antique enough to
have drawn a sword for Prince Charles,
and whose memory was well stored with
the legends of the neighborhood where he
now spent his last years, after a long service in the army. It was a very pretty
sight to see the tournaments in which he
engaged at chess with Mary Wincott. His
strategy was by no means so good as we
may hope it had been in the days of his
military youth. Perhaps he thought more
of his opponent than was quite compati-
ble with the confidence in his own powers,
which is so necessary an element of victory. It was certainly wonderful to see
how much surprised he appeared to be
when the flashing eyes and pearly teeth
shone for a moment between the lovely
lips opposite to him, laughed in his face,
and "Check Queen!" rang from the
round throat of "little Miss Mary," as he
called her. His tall frame, bowed with

years, and clothed in a handsome dress-
ing-gown, below which he wore a long
crimson velvet waistcoat, would stretch
forward, and then the fine old head, with
the white locks brushed carefully forward
in the old style, the fine curve of the
prominent nose, and white mustache and
beard, would bend over the board, and
then look gravely up into Mary Wincott's
face, and he would say :

"By George, I believe you've got me
this time!" and she, with a wealth of
darkened, cloudy locks, shaken back from
her straight and splendid brows, would
let the starlight of her great blue eyes
illume her perfectly molded and happy
countenance, and then she would sweetly
say :

"Never mind, Colonel McLain, you
will win next time."

Yes, indeed, it was a sight well worth
seeing when the head of the old man and
the head of the girl were bent toward

each other in that joyous antagonism, which made both, first so serious and then so merry, as they exchanged gracious little courtesies on the result of the game. To be sure, the combat generally ended one way only, and Beauty prevailed as usual over Valor; but Valor's chivalry made glorious his defeat, and Beauty's gracious. smiles and condolence made beautiful her victory. An artist who was one of the party staying at the house made sketches of the pair so engaged; but he never produced anything worthy of his theme, and the subject remains one which, if well rendered, would make the fortune of a painter equal to the task.

"Miss Mary, you don't mean to say you wish to scramble over all those rocks that guard the cave's mouth?"

"Yes, indeed, I do, Colonel, if your son will allow me: for although we don't walk so much in America as English girls do here, yet it seems to me that your climate makes walking pleasant, for it is never either too hot or too cold."

"Well, I hope they will take good care of you," said the old man; and one of the young guests forthwith exclaimed that if Miss Máry let him, he would answer for it that she would "not come to grief."

"You see I shall have plenty of guides and guards," she answered, laughing. "But is the way there so very difficult?"

"Yes," said Mr. McLain, "this cave, and others near it, have been used by smugglers even in quite recent times, because it is difficult to get at them. I believe that very many gallons of excellent whisky have, even within the last twenty-five years, been brought out of that place. During the winter gales, when a strong wind is beating the surf in from the west, and the great swelling rollers of the Atlantic are hurled against the cliffs, no Revenue vessel can approach; and from the landward side it is always easy for

the smugglers, or rather the lawless whisky brewers, to watch the few paths over
the moorlands, so as to give notice of any
person's approach. If strangers are in the
district it is soon known, and when there
are none to landward these robbers of
Her Majesty's Excise chest can be quite
sure that 'the coast is clear,' for no vessel
could at such time approach the shore.
Then descending the cliff and skirting the
boiling surf, which at flood-tide, or even
half-tide, effectually shuts out all prying
eyes even in fine weather, the smugglers
can go securely to work and get a lot of
work done before morning, when the tide
having turned to ebb they can carry out
their stuff, concealing it among the rocks
until it be safe for one of their boats to
take it away by water, or until it can be
carried inland."

"Why, how romantic!" cried Miss
Mary.

"Yes," said McLain. "You can't im-

agine a sight more weird than a high tide
on such a night, a moon silvering the
mighty surge as it lifts itself to break in
foam and send its hollow roar far along
the rocks and into the great caves. A
baffled Government vessel may be standing perhaps off and on outside as a phan-
tom in the gray of the further ocean.
And within the arched vaults of the cavern you may fancy the busy figures of
the smugglers crossing and recrossing the
sandy floor of the immense grotto, their
fires rapidly distilling the 'dew,' knowing
that for many hours their retreat is sealed
from any human eye, for no sign of their
work by light or sound can be seen or
heard from without. They make the best
of the time, and labor hard through all
the night hours, so that by the morning
there may be something 'well worth the
drinking.' As the firelight flickers on the
rough and curving walls and the sea winds
move the ferns that hang in plume-like

groups from the ledges, and the smoke from the secret stills floats over the half-illuminated scene, one might imagine that preparations were being made for deeds far more evil and mysterious than the making of a few wholesome 'nightcaps' for old men like my father there. It always seems to me that the punishment for such work is even now far too heavy, though it is nothing to what it was in the old days when to see a smuggler was to fire at him 'straightaway.'"

"If you go, mind you, bring me back some whisky for a nightcap," said old Colonel McLain, " but you'll have to start early. Had we not better be thinking about our beds now?"

Thus the happy party began to break up, as the ladies wished good-night to the gentlemen; but to these a cigar with more talk seemed indispensable, and they begged the aged Colonel not to retire so soon, but to give them for a little while

longer the benefit of his presence and conversation.

"Ah," he said, "I am too old. I will
leave you now, gentlemen." But his good
nature was not proof to their entreaties,
and he was wheeled near the fire, where
he declared it was a shameful dissipation
on his part to remain up so late, saying
he was nearly eighty years of age. They
declared that this could not be, and that
he was younger in mind than any of
them.

"I began to get old when most of you
were not born, and my hair was gray
when you were babes, although there is
none now."

"I wish I had as much still on my
head," said a very bald young man of
forty. "I've tried to prevent it going,
and concealed the alarming deficiency
by putting it over the bare places, but it
was all of no use." He quoted the epi-
gram:

"Our hair, when youth's before us, see
  Brushed back. Life's ours, we laugh !
When forward brushed, be certain we
  Look back on more than half !"

"You are too kind to an old man,"
smiled the Colonel. "But it is not long
since that an excursion like that you will
make to-morrow would have delighted
me. Long as my days have been, however, I have never seen reason to believe
in any of the bogies said to haunt men in
caverns or elsewhere." He declared that
although he had heard of such in the
underground places near this, he had not
thought of this matter at all, so lightly
did he regard the legends and superstitions of the people. Who did not know
that in every big hole in the ground
throughout all Celtic Scotland and all
Celtic Ireland there was either a mysterious piper or a strange harper? Who has
not heard of the piping or harping in the
dimmest corners, of musicians who retired

as mortals entered their haunts, and
marched away playing their melodies
until they went too far away into the
roots of the mountains to be heard any
more? "Nobody but a fool would repeat
such blethers," and he would be ashamed
of any one who did so.

Miss Mary certainly would not have
her pleasant dreams of her excursion on
the morrow dashed with any subterranean
nightmares—and she fell to sleep thinking, like a fanciful child, as in truth she
was, of the enchantment of entering the
nether world, which was one not of awe
and darkness to her mind, but an illu-
mined and endless procession of fairies,
who carried miniature torches in such
numbers that the place wherein they
moved sparkled like a huge diamond cor-
uscation. Each pendent form and mossy
ledge near the entrance of such abodes
were but resting-places for the pygmies
that must come, bearing deeply interest-

ing messages to the little inhabitants from others in like fortunate dwellings in far-off lands. It seemed probable that such messages took the love and state missives with greater speed, and by the shorter routes of the upper air, than could the sprites, who might communicate with distant places through the earth passages, which surely must exist. The rock-dove's wing traveled faster than could the little legs of the mountain elves, however strong these last might be, who acted no doubt as carriers for the little fairies, whose dignity could not allow them to do more than bear lights and hold councils.

With such delicious dreams Mary fell asleep, all eagerness for the excursion of the morrow. But the younger McLain, although he said nothing of the things he had heard in regard to the spot they were to visit, would not have laughed at the report that had reached his ears. It might be true that it had been the inter-

est of smugglers to make the superstitious
people about them believe the place to
be haunted. That they did so there could
be no doubt. But he had once himself
seen something there which he could not
explain, except upon the general supposi-
tion that things were visible to him which
were not visible to others. Yet he did
not like to think himself gifted in any
unusual way. Every circumstance that
had made him suspect himself to be so
had been most unwelcome to him, and he
tried to drive away the very thought.
The curious thing was that the smugglers
themselves were said to be so suspicious
of what they called their workshop that
they did not like to go there except in
bands of some strength, and not one of
them would have ventured, at least so it
was said, to sleep there alone. He said
nothing, knowing that the result of saying something would be either that he
would be " chaffed " by others or that he

2

would make them uncomfortable. As it
was, one of his friends had already told
him that he considered him to be uncanny.
There was little wonder at the friend's
opinion. This is what had happened.
The friend and McLain were sitting together, one windy day in the summer, in
the house where the present party had
assembled. McLain had been half doz-
ing, for the weather was hot, and his companion was reading a newspaper, when
suddenly, "without rhyme or reason," as
the phrase goes, McLain started up, rushed
in great agitation to the window, and
shouted, as though to an imaginary crew:

"Down with the sails, down with them,
down — d'ye hear? down, down with
them!" and then, after a breathless
pause, with the utmost distress of voice,
"By ——! she's gone!" and then, when
his companion looked at him in amaze-
ment, he was still all trembling. I could
only say that he thought he must have

been dreaming, but he had seen a ship go down in a squall. And sure enough, not so far from where they were, but far out of sight of any mortal eyes looking from that house, a ship had thus sunk. Yet McLain knew naught of this vessel. It was nothing to him. He knew none on board, and only saw the vision.

CHAPTER II.

"O MY, I wish you were coming also, Colonel," said Miss Mary on the following morning, when after breakfast she went to see the old man in his room.

"Well, I wish I were, by Mary," he said, and continued, "You see that I can use an old oath or affirmation, Miss Mary, as you do, and I like to use it with your pretty name."

"How? I use an oath! My! Colonel, what are you saying now?"

"It is as I say," replied the old man with a smile, "when you say 'O my,' you use the old oath or form of invocation 'O Mary,' shortened into 'O M'y.' It used to be considered enough in these parts in the old Catholic days, but now it is a pretty exclamation, more honored in America than here."

"Well, I never knew that," laughed the girl. "Fancy that I should have to come all this way to know the meaning of an expression I have heard used all my life. O my! How odd!"

"Well, if you check my Queen, I didn't want to check your 'O Mary,' Miss Mary," and away she went to complete her preparations for the expedition.

It was a long drive, but greatly to be enjoyed. The house in which they had met was situated near the sea and at the mouth of a wide glen flanked by towering hills, various in form and covered on their lower slopes with oak and hazel copse, and above the natural wood with heath that shone purple as the bloom on the serried ranks of the plants caught the eye. The color of the hills was also re-markable, for red rocks made the morn-ing and evening sunlight seem almost unnaturally ardent in hue, while on the scarred and broken crests above a white rock gleamed snowlike on the summits of the highest hills. Mary, an artist by nature and by practice, was enchanted with the beauty of this coloring, and asked:

"How is it that the rocks up there look almost like snow, they are so white, while all around are the brown and purple or darker tints, and it is only white there against the sky? It looks as if a little of that foam that fringes the blue of the sea where it breaks quietly on the rocks of the shore had been by some mysterious agency floated away up to the tops of the mountains."

"Yes," answered young McLain, "that is one of the curiosities of this part of the world, and it is the result of the work both of the sea and of fire or great earth upheavals. All that white stuff that you see two or three thousand feet above our heads lay once on the ocean sands, and,

with the wonderful alchemy of the salt
depths, or it may be after the water had
been drained away and the surface raised,
the earth and sand became like flint, hardened and whitened by the quartz so that
each little grain of sand looked twice his
age because blanched and fixed to the
next grain. And among these grains the
sea-worms had worked, and one can see
the channel each creature made. There
they are in millions, filled in with quartz-
ite stuff, but plainly apparent. The old
sea floor with all its teeming life pilloried
for ever and lifted high into heaven's
face."

"Well, that's a very grand but very terrible idea, to have had such upturnings of
the earth," said Mary, thoughtfully, "and
.you have nothing now in the way of vol-
canoes nearer than Iceland, have you?"

"No," McLain answered, "but all the
neighboring country to the south of us is
covered with traps and basalt and every

evidence of fearful volcanic eruption. Underneath their crust of lava you sometimes find the leaves and stems of the plants that were buried by the fiery fluid or shower of hot ash. There must have been beautiful lakes surrounded by trees like those now growing in Japan, for we find them imbedded in mud, now turned to sandstone and hardened clay—preserved so that you can trace each tendril and leaf nerve, each delicate edge and vein network, saved from the crushing of the superincumbent mass of lava, by the friendly silt of the quiet pool into which they had fluttered down from the trees they had once covered."

Mary looked up with deep respect in her fresh blue eyes to the cliffs and abrupt rocks along the shore, the lovely lines of . her eyebrows rising in a gentle curve of wonder at what she heard, and the dusky rose tints of her cheek deepening with the interest of the revelation of an age far

older than the dimmest and darkest, and
most distant she had ventured to imagine.

The road as they traveled on became
wilder and wilder, now skirting some deep
bay on a ledge so immediately overhang-
ing the sea, that from the carriage they
could look down into the depths of green
gray crystal, where often a lobster trap
set floating on the tide, could be seen; or
the more graceful forms of cormorant,
seamew, and even Sheldrake and Eider
Duck be for a moment discovered around
some rocky promontory, before the birds
took wing or dived to avoid the dangers
of Mary's eyes. How often she had pitied
the poor eider duck, when as a child she
had been told that men took their feathers
and soft down to make into pillows and
quilts! And here were the actual birds,
as she fancied! No, they could not be the
same, for they had evidently plenty of
feathers remaining, and there were the
horrid young men of the party, one in her

carriage, and others in the next, "dying" as they said "to have a shot at those fellows," and she devoutly hoped they would have nothing of the kind. When the carriage way ran along these terraces she would look with awe at the precipitous masses that arose wall-like on the land side, leaving often but just room for the wheels to find safety on the narrow space left at their foot, and then she would breathe more freely when the rock walls retired a little inland, so that a steep turf slope intervened between herself and them, and it was not so evident as it seemed a minute or two before, that a piece of the cliff, loosened by winter frosts or summer rains, would, if it broke off and descended, crush them all to atoms.

The driver had delighted to point out places where huge masses had come off the cliff face, and, thundering down, had demolished a portion of the road be-

neath. He had had a narrow escape himself once, he declared, and his horse could
afterward hardly be persuaded to traverse
the dangerous passage, and even now was
all of a shake when he approached it.
The driver evidently wanted to make a
hero of himself and his horse, but still it
was a relief not to be obliged to keep an
eye in the air and one on the water, and
to feel free to keep both for the view of
the sparkling Atlantic, as it came flowing
in between islet after islet to caress the
shore, which had for countless years bid-
den it at once a welcome and a defiance.
And there where the beach was more
shelving, great beds of the magnificent
Laminaria could be observed, making
purple the blue of the water, where the
waving fronds of sea tangle remained
covered, or where the tide had left them,
the broad brown banners lying piled together, with their array of colored folds
glistening in the sunlight. There, next to

the green of the grass, made more vivid by
contrast with the gray and lichen-grown
bowlders, was the bright yellow band of
the shoreweed—sometimes showing also a
tawny red—to set off the laughing azure of
the calm deep beyond. Where the group of
flat topped rocks showed above the flood,
what round heads were there which kept
swimming about, as if a boat's crew had
been shipwrecked, and had rather enjoyed
the sensation, determining to make the
most of their luck in being cast away on
such a charming coast, and still desirous
of contemplating its charms from a little
distance, and so seemed to be amusing
themselves for some time longer in the
water before coming to shore? No, they
could not be men, for they went down too
often, and reappeared at places a diver
could not reach. No, they were seals;
and presently one came up close to the
shore, looked with round black eyes
solemnly at the carriage, and then shut

its nostrils and sank slowly down, the pug nose disappearing the very last, and then his native curiosity being unsatisfied he came up again, and not content with giving a wink with one of his eyes, he raised himself breast high, to have a long stare.

One of the party said "I killed two of them the other day, and have ordered several specimens of their skins."

Mary gave the speaker such a look of horror and disgust that he wished he had bitten his lips through before he had made such an avowal, and heard her indignant—

"Well, I think the man that can shoot those harmless and beautiful things deserves to have the fire returned by the friends of outraged innocence."

"Oh, but, Miss Mary," pleaded the peccant sportsman, "indeed, indeed, they aren't such guileless things as you imagine. They play the devil with the salmon, and I myself have seen one of them pass

under my boat in hot pursuit of a poor
salmon, who deserved your pity, when I
lay on my oars floating in shallow water."

Miss Mary did not look convinced, and
would only vouchsafe, "Well, they are
worth any number of salmon; of that I
am sure."

Turning a headland which sheltered a
long fiord, or loch, from the outer ocean,
they came in sight of the rocky islands
of the Hebrides, which with great variety
of form lay out to sea at distances vary-
ing as much as did the shapes they presented to the eye. The largest had hills
of considerable height and of picturesque
ruggedness of outline, which here seemed
as though terraced by the hand of man,
so regular were the flats which terminated
in abrupt precipices, like huge steps set
in the silver sea. Mary had seen the
fairy isles of Capri and Ischia that lie off
Naples, but she did not miss the wondrous rose tints which so often mantle

them, as she gazed at these northern isles.
They had a beauty of coloring all their
own, and she did not feel tempted to
make comparisons.   She had seen (for
what does a young American not see now-
adays?) those last and largest of the isles
of the Archipelago of the Adriatic, the
little ocean realms of Corfu and Zante,
the "flowers of the Levant," lift their
sloping sides and olive-crowned heights
over the straits which are guarded on the
Turkish shore by the long line of the Al-
banian Highlands.   If she had compared
what she now looked upon with those
scenes of the East, she might perhaps
have regretted that here the softness and
charm that comes alone with wavy woods
was absent, and she did indeed say to
young McLain:

"I hear of deer forests in the island,
but these must be away inland?"

He told her that the use of the word
"forest" dates from a long way back in

the history of this country, when a natural growth of oak and fir and smaller trees covered the land.

"There are bits," he said, "of the old Scots fir forests left, but they are chiefly in rather inaccessible places where the wants of the needy and scanty population of old Scotland did not tempt their destruction. Wherever there were people crowded in their poverty and cold in the valleys, there the woods disappeared, gradually cut down for the fires in the huts of the natives or burned by carelessness. It is astonishing how a fire will run during a hot summer. You would imagine that the trees would have been too green and wet here. But this is not the case, and in a dry season I have known a whole hill-side of nice wood burned up by the careless leaving of a fire lit to amuse a picnic party. 'Wooded Caledon' the Romans called Scotland, and wherever you cut a peat from the mosses, or drain these, you will see the roots of trees, sometimes of large oaks. I have got excellent pieces of bog oak cut from large trunks found deeply imbedded in the peat. They are very heavy, these fallen and sunken trees, to drag out, for they are quite water-logged. One must cut trenches round them, and let the wood dry slowly before it is used, otherwise it all goes into splinters, and is useless for ornament or furniture making. The color is a capital blue-black, and if you want to be sure of a bit keeping quite sound for carving purposes, the best plan is to keep it for a month or more in warm water, so that the cold water gets driven out of it, and then to keep it for some weeks in a mixture of glue and warm water, when the glue is carried into the heart of the wood and solidifies it, making it quite firm enough for any delicate chiseling."

Miss Mary told him she had once seen

3

a spring in America that was so full of flinty stuff that any wood put into it became like agate in a short time.

"Ah, we can't match America in anything, Miss Wincott."

"Oh, yes, but you do," she replied warmly. "In the old memories you have delights for the mind we have not got, and then the color here of the sun, glimpses seen among white mists, and the purple and dark blue shadows, and the exquisitely soft and tender greens are things we find new to us."

Now before them, as they drove along, the great cliff receded inland, and on the slanting ledges, a mile or so wide, was luxuriant pasture, so that they looked over the sward to where it fell to the water, that flashed in little lines and spots and points of light. These verdant slopes, wherever they were steepest, had marks of old dikes or rough walls intersecting them in every direction. They were the marks of the ancient divisions, and very minute divisions many of them seemed, between the old croft lands, and they extended from the cliff of the sea to the foot of a high wall of mountain, which must have sheltered their owners from the eastern blasts of winter. There were half-a-dozen nicely-built new cottages along the road, and a large, white farm- house among the green patches of the old crofter cultivation. Large numbers of sheep could be seen on the hill-sides, and a fine herd of cattle below wandered at will, feeding on the rich grasses.

"Oh, what a place to live in!" ex- claimed Mary. "Rather lonely, perhaps; but with a friend or two, and the sea to cheer one, that wouldn't matter—for a time," she added, as if doubtful how far her exclamation might be taken as a real wish, and she might be left to enjoy the solitude.

"Well," said McLain, "the people must

have been cheerful enough here at one time, and those that live in the houses you see get enough to eat, and are fortunate. But in the old days it was not so, and the sheep were poor and small. No drainage system was known, so that it was only where the rains fell off the land by reason of its steepness that cultivation was possible. The land was tilled by a hand plow. A century ago there were about forty to fifty souls living here. Then the potato was introduced from the south, where it had long been known. It was got, as you know, from your country. Well, the potato acted, strangely enough, as an ambassador to ask the people to go to America. But it did not do so at once. On the contrary, it said to them, 'Here I am come to remain with you—a fat, jolly bulb, and you can fatten on me and stay where you are.' So they feasted on him, and he seemed to thrive with them, and the people multiplied fast.

Why, in fifty years they had increased so
much that there were three times the
number living in the place. And then
the American envoy, the potato, suddenly found out that the climate was not
quite to his liking, and gave only black-
ened bulbs where before there had been
wholesome, creamy roots. The people
sickened and starved, and some were
helped to go to America, and they wrote
home that there was plenty and no potato
disease. Then came a mania for a resi-
dence on your big continent, and the
owners of the land got frightened that
all their people would leave them; and
many tried to make them stay, but in
vain. They would go. Their children
are rich enough now, and the owners of
the land have found out that they could
manage also with fewer tenants."

"It seems sad that they could not have
remained in their own country, although,
to be sure, I should not have been a free

American myself if my ancestors had not been progressive and left the old country," said Mary, her eyes becoming cloudy and thoughtful, and continued : " I have heard it said that the rights of the people were taken from them, and that the land that was theirs became the laird's."

McLain would not for one moment allow this.

" That is a piece of agitator's lying," he said warmly, " got up by them for purposes of a little cheap election popularity. But I think they have found themselves mistaken. The people are in the long run too honest and sensible to believe that they can take at will other men's goods. Of old the laird was a terrible autocrat. It is quite true that unless he wanted what he called ' loyal ' tenants, he did not displace those on the soil, because they were his own people to some extent, and it was not natural that he should do so. But if in troubled times they went against the side he espoused, they were moved and others put in their places. This happened in our mixed and vexed history often enough. The obedience they had to render to their chief and chieftains was absolute, and the continuance in their lands, and the enjoyment of them, according to their rude fashion, was theirs because they gave their chief warlike service. He had only to hold up his little finger, or more practically and literally go to a kirk and blow a horn, and his men had to go with him, the next moment, if he so willed it, to cut the throat of the nearest neighboring chief and his folk in the next glen. That is fact. And yet with the fiction that the lands were not the property of the chiefs, who have always exercised the rights of property over them, our sapient legislators have given to the occupiers the houses built by myself and others. The result of course is that we can build no longer for our friends,

and must leave them to shift for themselves."

"O, Mr. McLain! I am sure you are
glad that the poor people have their share
of houses and lands," said Mary.

"Yes, indeed I am, Miss Mary; but I
fear the general effect of such laws trans-
ferring what has been one man's to another's possession, .will be that most people will take care to put no houses on land
that may be thus taken from them. They
will say to the poor: 'Now you have been
put in possession as owner of that I gave
you to make you comfortable, and you
must look to the Government and not to
me for further help.' The Government
will say: 'No, we have done it for a few,
but we can't do it for all, nor can we continue to help the person to whom we have
given the land, to. live upon it.' The
wisest plan would have been to have made
laws against wrongful use of legal powers
in the case of the poor, instead of putting

the poor in a position of temporary and false independence that can last for a short time only, and then leave him in a position worse off than before, when he could look to the landlord as a friend as well as a neighbor."

"I should help them at all times," said sweet Miss Mary; "but I have known many, like your Scotchmen, who would not do so certainly if the gentlemen who had left the people on their land were to be so fined for their goodness. It is easy to exercise charity at other people's expense. Those talkers would act meanly if they themselves had to lose anything by their talk. Perhaps that is so. Anyhow you would not wish to fight your neighbors over those hills now, Mr. McLain, so you don't want the war service of the crofters."

"We should like some of them to serve in the army against a national enemy, but they won't serve either their chiefs or the

Queen in her army now, and even in the
old days it was difficult enough to persuade them to come forward, for instance,
for the French war."

"Why, that's the time of our war with
you, the war of Independence," said Miss
Mary, mischievously, "and if they had
been all persuaded to serve, we should
have a good many more bad potatoes
planted among us, I guess."

"Ours are not bad potatoes," laughed
Mr. McLain, "but all peasants, if they
have a hearth, don't like to leave it. In
France you have to have forced service,
or conscription, on this ground, that the
men who dislike most the military service
are the men who can call some land their
own. We found it too difficult, as I say,
in the old days to get them to turn out,
great as our power over them was, and I
doubt if you planted these hills and valleys thickly with people, first, whether
many would stay, because the demands

for comfort are far higher now, and they would not be satisfied; secondly, whether those who did stay and were content to live in places where none but the least enterprising would remain, could be persuaded to contribute a contingent to the army. Some of the crowding of the crofting population that took place after the war was in consequence of the cutting up of good farms into small bits to accommodate men who would serve only on the promise of the possession of such land after the campaign."

"Well, now, tell me something of their belief, besides their faith in the virtues of doing nothing," she said. "Are they very superstitious?"

"Not more so than most uneducated people, and perhaps less so than many who are highly educated. The things that are told of saints and others were taught them by the most educated men of old time, whose nonsense can be heard

any day at the present, if one takes up a
church book. Of course, there's the Evil
Eye. I have never been in any country
where that was not more or less firmly
believed in. In Ireland they put a piece
of bent stick over the lock of a door when
they leave their cabin to prevent the Evil
Eye or hobgoblin from entering. A friend
of mine used to put up at the house of a
lady who had a farm situated near a road
he often had to take. She used hospi-
tably to give him a night's lodging as he
passed. One day to his surprise as he
left her door she said goodby, and that
she must request him not to call again,
as each time he had come she had lost a
cow, a horse, a pig, a hen, or some creature she had owned, through death. It
must be my friend's evil eye that did the
mischief. She was very sorry, but she
must thank my friend not to call again.
It is always considered unlucky to start
on a voyage, however short, in a boat un-

less you turn the boat three times round
with the sun. This has no doubt nothing
to do with the evil eye, but it is a remnant
of the ancient sun worship. But ill luck
attaches itself in their minds to any boat
from which a man has fallen overboard
and been lost. Would you believe it, I
once told some men that they might pur-
chase a boat at my expense. They went
and chose a very good one. Some ma-
licious agitators did not like them to ac-
cept a boat from me, and they started a
cock and bull story that a man had been
lost from the vessel. From the moment
this lie was spread among them not a man
of the crew which had been got together
would touch the boat. They actually left
it to lie and rot on the beach, and some
more sensible person offered a few pounds
for it, bought it, as none of the people of
the place would do anything with her; and
she is now in his hands giving an excellent return in the fish that her lowland

crew take. It is amazing that our people should thus listen to strange men and still stranger women. But there are other bees in other people's bonnets, and we must hope that they who have known us from childhood will return in affection to us, who have for generations been their real friends. But it is not their superstition, but their old predatory habits that the tempters play upon in speaking to them against us now. If they could only be got to believe that the evil eye and bad luck would follow them if they broke up the friendship their fathers had with ours, they would never think of turning against us. Even if gold were at the end of the cave we are about to visit, no human persuasion would tempt them to enter it after dark alone."

CHAPTER III.

LEAVING the carriages at the large, white farmhouse, wraps and luncheon-baskets were consigned to the ghillies, and a delightful walk undertaken over the pastures that topped the sea-cliffs. Orchises and little pansies flecked the grass, and where any natural knoll, too rough for the herbage, had broken the surface, there the heather seeds had dropped and flourished, and the hum of bèes in the deep red bells and minute purple flowerets told of the grateful gathering of unenvied wealth. Now the path skirted the very edge of the abrupt wall, which rose close to the line of refluent sea-water, and although there was no wind and no lashing wave, yet the heart-beat of the mighty deep, sent, in measured undulations, shining masses that almost insensibly swelled and laved with an ampler flood the jagged stones and sandy coves, while a low murmur, as though of pleasure, rose upon the air; only every now and then a little flush of darker blue mantled, for an instant, the surface, where a breath of wind had wandered from the mountains inland, and had fallen over the cliff, and struck with a light "flurry" upon the waters.

Mary would have liked to lie down on the perfumed bank to gaze for hours on the grandeur of the coast which dipped, headland beyond headland, into those turbulent depths. She had seated herself, but rose, saying, "Man is always in a hurry when he should rest, and generally thinking when he should be acting," for she was told that the tide would soon be too high for their purpose if they delayed. She left, with a sigh, the place

made to look yet more restful by her re-
pose, and found that they had been led
to a break in the rock wall, and that close
to where they stood, a very steep, but
still quite practicable slope of turf, made
a descent tolerably easy. The only one
of the party who would not venture it
was an elderly Italian, who looked down
the steep green stairs of turf, shook his
head over the abyss, and murmured re-
peatedly, "Imposs! imposs!" Nothing
could persuade him to attempt the task,
even although the ladies offered him their
fair shoulders as a support for his hands.
"Imposs," as they then called him, was
left at the top of the bank, looking over
the path, "like an old mare over a gate,"
as one of the others remarked, with more
truth than politeness.

A scramble brought them all safely to
the bottom, and then began a more difficult part of the road, for the little space
left between rock and sea was strewed

4

with huge bowlders rolled up by the ice
in past ages, and fragments of rock detached and tumbled from above. These
lay in confusion, piled one above the
other, strewed in wondrous disorder, little pools left by the tide scattered among
them, where their lower surfaces were
decked with the little pyramids of the
limpet, and scarred white with the crusts
of barnacle and serpula. The men had
plenty to do to get the women over the
rough obstructions of the shore, and they
all paused, breathless with their climbing,
where a rough table of stone gave them
a comparatively flat platform whereon to
take breath. Above them, over the precipice, streamed a little burn, coming from
what seemed a great height, and gradually getting thinner and thinner in its
volume until it reached the broken rocks
below, a mere streak of foam-white spray,
showing through its veil the red and gray
of the stone beyond, and the green tufts

of fern and ivy which clung to that over-
hanging wall. And now, beyond a last
giant buttress, they were told that the
object of their journey lay. They had,
however, been so careful to arrive as the
tide was retiring that they had come too
soon, and were obliged to wait, because
the road around the foot of the angle of
rock was still flowing knee-deep. A wild
pigeon or two flew in before them into
the recess they desired to reach, and they
envied the birds their wings. A little patience was, however, easily learned ˙ on
that glorious spot, and soon the white
and green and muddy pebbles showed
shining wet, for they were still kissed by
the lips of the sea, but the sun disputed
their possession, and the travelers could
tread on them. Just round the corner
the whole of the immense opening of the
cave showed itself to their astonished
eyes. Far away overhead the cliff broke
into a vast portal, whose rugged and ir-

regular arch grew gradually lower and
lower as the aperture deepened inward.
This covered approach to the actual entrance of the cave was paved with many-
colored pebbles, while the rock in terraced ledges rose grandly on each side
as they stood within. The roof above
was more beautiful than could have been
any closed vault; for, open to the sun
and sea air through its wide and lofty
entrance, it appeared like the avenue to
some mystic Egyptian temple, where the
perspective makes the walls close in and
in, until the opening to the cave itself
leads in the distance to the narrow entrance which guards the sacred halls of
the secret and inner fane.

Mary, with the impetuosity of her girl-
ish character, sped on over the pavement
of small stones that made walking laborious, and, followed by her companions,
stood for a while beneath the ragged
lintel of the door of the cave vault; there

the archway was only about thirty feet in height. Looking behind, she saw the blue line of the sea's horizon, formed by the rocks, and inclosing on its farthest verge an island, which seemed a mere mote in that intense light which shone on the outer world. Before her loomed a great space of darkness, where the rocky ceiling rose into impenetrable gloom. The floor still rose slightly, but not with so decided an incline, and it was now sand and not a confused collection of rounded stones on which she stood. Her eyes gradually became more accustomed to the gloom, and she saw how extensive was the natural hall into which she had ventured.

"Oh, look what nice soft sand; and there are flat stones to make tables for our lunch," she said, and pointed to some blocks that gleamed shadowy white some forty yards away.

She moved on to them, and when nearer

she saw, or thought she saw, seated on
them a man. The figure, if she could
trust her eyes in the obscurity, was that
of an old man. He was clad in a brown
or dark-looking long coat, and had a
white beard, and his hat was on his head,
a battered wide-brimmed cloth hat that
concealed a good deal of the face. She
was startled for a moment, and looked
toward her companions as if asking if
they should camp there, as others seemed
to be there before them. But when she
looked again the figure had moved, and,
thinking that it must only be some tourist visiting the cavern as she and her
friends were, she sat down on the sand,
and soon the baskets were emptied of
the luncheon, and a laughing group made
the corks fly, and jokes and merriment
reigned. They sat with their backs to
the darkness, and fronting the entrance,
so that the cheerful day made a deep
shaft of light strike along the floor al-

most to their feet. The glare was so
rarefied by the space it had to pass that
they could look forth undazzled through
that little arch, to where the island
floated, far away. If any person had
attempted to pass out they must therefore, of course, have seen him, and toward
the end of their repast, Mary said in a
low voice to her neighbor, that she wondered what had become of the old gentleman who had been sitting so near where
they then were when they first entered.

"Old gentleman! there is nobody here
surely but ourselves," said she, and this
statement was echoed by those who were
sure that there could be nobody, and that
there had been nobody there, or they
would have seen them. Only young Mc-
Lain backed Mary's remarks, and said
that he, too, had positively seen a man
move away into the darker parts of the
cave. He added, laughing:

"If it isn't a tourist, it must be some

belated smuggler." He, too, had noticed the white beard and the long brown coat. " Well," he said, in the undertone in which their conversation had been carried on, for they knew not if they might not be overheard, " if it's a smuggler we'll soon find him, for this great vault is as round as a kettle, and the main corridor that leads out of it farther on into the hill, ending in another smaller hall, has no side passages that I have ever seen or heard of. Light the candles and lanterns, and we'll soon show you the end of any mystery there may be here."

All started to their feet, and a number of lights, little glow-worms, searched the moist walls, and peered into any crannies that appeared. The sandy floor rose higher and higher, until it ended in a ridge under the place where the rock ceiling again descended from its height to within thirty feet of the floor. Beyond this ridge a wide passage led and past more big stones, until a slight descent a hundred yards farther brought them to the room described by McLain. The farther end of this was blocked by pieces of rock detached from the roof.

They had come across no person, and now that they could speak without fear of being overheard, Mary was often merrily told that she had been long enough in Scotland, for she had begun to share the second sight McLain was reported to possess. She was certainly much puzzled, and so was he, at the absence of any proof of their statement, and they answered little, and seemed to regard the matter more seriously than did the others. So much was this the case that the attempt at badinage on the subject died away, and they left the cave far more silent than when they entered it. But their spirits revived with the renewed exercise of the exertion of the scramble over the fearfully rough shore; the young men were happy enough in helping Mary over the rugged obstacles, and they would encourage her to rest and stand on some big stone, where they could admire her as she stood above them, her young figure appearing to their gaze more beautiful than that of any Grecian goddess, as she remained awhile looking to seaward, her hand, as it leaned on a long staff of hazel, raised above her head, the masses of her dark hair showing in abundance under a blue flat "boori," or basque cap, her rounded and firm chin, clear cut lips, and nostrils taking in the salt breath of the ocean, with a delight that her great and happy eyes made glorious to behold.

But all good things must come to an end, including the chance of seeing a beautiful girl motionless, and having the luck to be allowed to stare at her without being rude; for now the top of the cliff had to be gained. There they found their sedentary friend, "Old Imposs," as they

called him, waiting for their return, de-
claring that he had had a much better
time of it than they, but, by the by, had
they any lunch left, for he had quite for-
gotten that he had none in his pockets
when they went down to the shore, and
he had begun to envy the cormorants
below him, for he had seen a lot of them
on a rock taking a wash in the water, en-
joying a most substantial meal on fish,
that he had begun to feel hungry enough
to eat raw.

The ladies rather unkindly declared
he deserved nothing until he got back to
the farm-house, but one of the ghillies
was seen to keep back alone with him,
and it was feared he had obtained a sur-
reptitious supply of whisky and biscuit,
for he did not mention the cormorants
again. Young McLain soon made a pre-
text for telling him and the rest to pro-
ceed, as he decided to fetch something he
had accidently left on the shore, and wan-

dered back the way they had come. But
no sooner were they out of sight than he
reascended the grassy bank, and crept
onward along the cliff brink where heather screened the abyss, until he knew by
the lie of the land he stood immediately
over the cave. Here he lay down and
crept cautiously, as though stalking a
deer, and determined to remain unseen,
to the very brink. Parting the heather,
he looked cautiously down.

Nearly an hour had now elapsed since
they had left the cave, and looking down
upon the shore where the big bowlders
they had crossed with so much difficulty,
appeared no larger than a boy's toy marble, this is what he saw. It was nothing
very startling, but it was something that
puzzled him considerably.

A boat, with a small sail lying along
the thwarts, was being unfastened from a
tiny creek in the rocks below. This miniature cove must have been entirely con-

cealed from any one climbing along the rough shore, unless it was accidentally stumbled upon. Besides, it lay beyond the approach to the cave.

Engaged in unfastening the boat, and working with evident energy to get it away before the tide yet receded farther, was a man. Unlike the person McLain and Mary thought they had seen in the darkness of the cavern, this person was evidently young and vigorous. McLain pulled out his field glass, and saw him as though he could have touched him. He had fair and fine hair, which had grown long over the forehead and back, and was bright and curly. On the crown of the head it seemed to have been cut shorter, as though for the sake of some wound. The youth was bareheaded. A new growth of young hair covered his chin and lip. He seemed nervous and hurried; his eyes were expressive enough, but the expression was one of some anxiety and tension of mind, enforced by a knitting of his brows and the quick motion of his hands, with which he often threw back the hair and dried his brow. Soon the painter was free, the little mast stepped, although the sail was not yet hoisted.

The young man jumped into the little craft, and soon shoved himself into the deep. Then he took the oars as he stood, and rowed for a while standing between the thwarts, in order to see ahead, for he seemed fearful of some rock or shallow. He did this slowly, but evidently quite at ease now that he was afloat and had caught the ebbing water. And as he slowly bent and swung forward, leaning on the oars, he paused at intervals, and his heart seemed to fill with joy, as, with head erect, he sang these strange words :.

" Out from the darkness, forth into light,
    From the vault of earth I go ;
The Rock-dove's neck but needs her flight
    From the cave, in the sun to glow,

So my soul, athirst for the open day,
   Moves aflame with the love Divine ;
O shelter me, shine on my ocean way,
   God ! with the angels nine.

" The devious tracks are passed at last,
   I see the heavens blue,
Thy love's great tide swings free and vast,
   And thrills the whole world through,
Unchanging, in its change, to fill
   With health the noisome mine ;
So come, Thou all-compelling Will,
   With Thy great angels nine.

" I sought to know Thy way through those
   Who make themselves as God ;
The worm that on his belly goes,
   Their sign—not Thy green sod—
Thy sunlight was not in their heart,
   Nor Thy great ways Divine ;
Thy breakers shatter their dull art,
   Thou need'st not angels nine !

" Priests spin their cobwebs, hiding truth,
   And weave their nets for power ;
One honest pulse of healthy youth
   Is worth their creed's long hour ;
Then forth to follow to the West,
   Thy great Sun's golden sign ;
Away with any man-made test,
   My soul's whole worship Thine ! "

The voice ascended clear and strong in
the calm evening air, and still the young
rower stood and propelled his craft in
the leisurely fashion with which he had
started. But soon a little breeze touched
the surface around him, and he stooped
to raise his sail. And McLain marveled
more and more who on earth he could be,
but refrained from hailing him, much as
he felt inclined to shout out a happy
journey to him—"merely for the fun," as
he said afterward, "of startling him."
But there fell no voice from the height to
surprise the youth. The quiet beauty of
this Western night would soon be around
him. A few cries from gulls, a few
splashes as a diver threw up his tail and
disappeared, or the sound of the watery
shock of the plunge after his prey of the
solan bird; the feathery "whisk" heard
at intervals from the place where the
little brook fell down the precipice, and
the more constant hollow whisper of the

tide along the shore, a sound that never •
allows an absolute silence, even on the
calmest day—these, and these alone, could
be heard when the song ceased.   The
dusky cobalt of the upper heavens became yet deeper, as the golden glory in
the west brightened, and ever brightened.
A few pennon-like streaks of cloud
glowed with an ethereal crimson, and in
varied lights of palest green, and saffron,
and blue, the sea shone responsive to the
light above.   The isles and islets afar
upon its breast assumed a deep sapphire
tint, and McLain's thoughts turned to the
Celtic legends of the Isles of the Blessed,
the Avilion whither the spirit of Arthur
passed at his death.   Where were they,
those "fortunate. isles?"   Where never
wind blew loudly, nor mortal grief could
come?   Would he or any man ever find
them? or could they ever be seen—for, in
the end, there would be "no more sea."
How then could there be any happy

5

shores in the West, he asked himself, half-smiling at the futility of his own thoughts. And as he so checked himself in his dreaming, he took another look through his glass at the voyager in the little boat. The sail was drawing the light air and he was fast leaving the land behind, and gliding quietly toward the blaze in the west; and McLain gazed again toward the sunset, and saw far down on the burning horizon what seemed to be the very isle of his desire. There it stood from out the opal-tinted deep, refulgent with more than mortal brightness. There rose a glittering shore with sudden peak and deep ravine, with splintered mountain ridge and glens glowing with the sheen of molten precious metals. Distinct and unmistakable, the strange land lay along the water, an Eldorado so clearly defined that the most skeptical eye could not doubt of its existence. The youth in the now distant boat appeared to see it, for he stood up and gazed westward, as though beholding the vision of wonder beyond the rough basaltic masses that broke through the ocean surface nearer to him. But now the night came on apace; the boat grew smaller and smaller. It was only the nearer and familiar and certainly material forms of the Hebrides that could be dimly distinguished in the gathering gloom, and McLain left his watch, puzzled and feeling decidedly superstitious, with a prevalent feeling that the mysterious young man had got a clew to a scent that had long escaped the most searching Celt, and had shipped himself off "for good," to the happy land, which none really deserved until they had grown to be at least four times as old as the young voyager, or three times as old as McLain himself.

CHAPTER IV.

THAT inland sea, ringed with its round-headed hills of yellow sand, called the Harbor of San Francisco, shone steel blue, as the usual cold wind blew upon it through the " golden gate "—the opening to the Pacific. In the carved court of the immense Palace Hotel, which in that city engulfs most of the travelers who arrive as fleeting birds of passage, the band made the white, wooden-columned colonnades of each of its many stories resound with a brazen din. There was an incessant banquet proceeding in the lower halls, where a never-ending *table d'hôte* attracted and surfeited people, who seemed to come from most of the civilized countries under the sun. In the luxurious upper rooms, little supper and dinner parties were being given ; and sometimes the purchases that had been made of curiosities in the city discussed, and the articles displayed.

There were many handsome shops in the straight streets which ran up and down the monstrous sand-hills, but the monotony of the things set out for the benefit of tourists was usually even greater than that of the streets and hills. Specimens of gold in dust; specimens of gold in crystals of pure yellow metal; specimens of gold in quartz, cut and polished; specimens of gold in nuggets, small and big. These were the forms that the San Francisco commercial enterprise exhibited as the chief novelties and peculiarities of the place, and some of the visitors had had enough of them. This was the case with a party which had just arrived from the Eastern States, and although tired with the long time spent

in the cars, had already seen most of the
sights of the city, including some of the
magnificent wooden-built houses of the
principal merchant princes, the park where
the sea-lions are shown, reposing their
ungainly carcasses on the stack of rocks
that jut out into the long rolling surge of
the Pacific. They were talking of an expedition to Montalto, where the Govern-
or's splendid herd of horses might be seen
by those who could present introductions
to him; but it was resolved that they had
not yet thoroughly "done" San Francisco, and a visit to the Chinese theatre,
in the Chinese quarter, would be something new at all events, and would show
them something unlike what they had
seen before. So the opera or academy
of music, as many towns in America love
to call that institution, was left for another day, and the carriages were ordered
to set the party down in the "Celestial's"
part of the city.

A very ill-formed part it was, with
many wooden houses, little better than
shanties, a contrast to the vast blocks of
handsome buildings of which most of this
city was built. To be sure, the preva-
lence of earthquakes, mild in character
as these generally are, might make many
a nervous person prefer a single storied
building to one containing many floors,
as escape would be easier; but there are
too many brick and stone buildings to
allow one to imagine that the occasional
danger exercises much influence on the
minds of the inhabitants. Along the
sides of the streets into which the party
now penetrated there were many low
shops and dingy counters, protected from
sun and rain by a roof of projecting
boards, supported from the floor of the
side-walk by posts, against which Chinese
loungers leaned, wearing the familiar pig-
tail, and clad in long, loose dresses of
black or dark blue. Usually there were

no shoes on their feet, but every now and then a richer man passed, his drapery of finer stuff, and white shoes on his feet, turned up at the toes like the prow of an old-fashioned boat.

The theatre itself was a long dark parallelogram, with a gallery, the ends of which nearest the stage were divided off into small partitions. Lamps of the most ordinary kind gave just enough light to enable persons entering to see their way to rough benches, which were always well filled with a crowd of Chinese workingmen. They sat very silently awaiting the commencement of the piece which had always been proceeding to develop its story during three or four of the preceding evenings. One peculiarity of the acting struck a stranger as curious when the acting began.

There was no attempt to keep the "wings" or sides of the stage free of those who were not acting, although they might have been friends of the actors. They indulged their curiosity as much as they chose, by standing in deep rows, and laughing or cheering the action of the drama.

Another peculiarity consisted in a band of musicians, if this term of flattery for a knot of men making hideous noises be permissible, being stationed in the very center of the stage. In front of them the actors who conducted the story recited their parts in a loose fashion, that suggested they were improvising as they went on. The applause from the audience was occasionally loud and hearty, especially was a droll fellow, who often came forward to make jokes, rewarded with plentiful laughter. There seemed to be only one woman in the cast, and all the other characters made love to her, a method of insuring "the unities" which allowed the play to be indefinitely protracted, and yet kept the interest circling round the lovely female, who, as far as the assemblage in the house was concerned, seemed to be the only Chinese woman in 'Frisco. There must have been others somewhere, but they were apparently not so clamorous for boxes and stalls as are their paler sisters of our race. There was no attempt at scenic decoration, although in more luxurious theatres it is said that this is being introduced. Like the plays of the classical day of Italy and Greece, and like those of our own Shakespeare, the diction was supposed to be entrancing enough without such meretricious attractions. And then, as the Chinese clown in shrill tones and with ludicrous gestures straddled on the stage front, and was every now and again succeeded by this single and singular woman, who had all the Chinese world at her feet, a light which did not come from the stage but from overhead made the audience look up, a shower of sparks fell among them, making them start to their feet, then came more sparks and a bright outflush of flame overhead. There was a quitting of the stage by those upon it, and men were soon heard tearing at the roof, which blazed up ever brighter and brighter. Then a babel of tongues that had begun as soon as the fire was seen was lost in loud cries of terror, and the panic-stricken Chinamen rushed to the entrance doorway below, while those in the galleries, who from their position were nearer the fire, and had at first observed it, were screaming at the top of their voices, dashing over each other, struggling to be first to reach the creaky stairway.

It was an appalling scene, for it was evident that the men above had done nothing to stop the misfortune, which now threatened irredeemable disaster. The party from the hotel had risen from where they sat, the chief figure among them being a father and daughter, who

stood holding each other's hands, pale
and silent amid the tumult, but really
terrified like the rest, for imminent death
appeared to stare them in the face. It
was evident that no egress was possible
by the door crammed with frantic struggling Chinamen.

Then suddenly a thoroughly Californian
figure, a man spare, and agile, and of
good stature, with a sombrero-like hat
on his head, and long fair hair showing
on his neck, sprang toward them, climbed
the railing that divided their portion of
the gallery from the pit below, and in a
moment had taken the old man's arm,
and hurried him and his daughter toward
the side wall. There at one corner was
a low door closed and fastened—a door
that none had looked for or observed.
This yielded at once to the weight of his
shoulder, and in another minute they
were all outside the burning building,
and on a roof whence they could reach

one of the veranda-like boardings over
the street side-walk.   Letting himself
down first, he bade them one after the
other leap down to him, and, receiving
them safely in his wiry arms, they found
themselves breathless, but unhurt, in the
roadway.

Mary Wincott, for it was she and her
father who had so narrowly escaped, was
pale enough still and trembled a good
deal, nor could she at first summon voice
to thank their guide, who now asked them
if they were at the Palace Hotel, in a
manner happy enough, but as though
trying to suppress the intense excitement
under which his voice labored.

"Well, I'll show you the way," he said,
in reply to their answer, and striding by
their side, with his wide hat framing a
handsome face, he said not another word
until they reached the hotel door, when
he saluted them, and would have left had
not Mr. Wincott pressed his hand, and

told him that he must ask him to come
again as soon as possible to receive their
thanks for his most opportune appearance
and assistance. A more impetuous mem-
ber of the group broke in.

"Why, yes, sir. If you hadn't come
we should all have been crisps by this
time."

The Californian smiled and said he
would have the pleasure of again calling, and, with a low bow to Miss Wincott,
departed. They met very soon again,
for the next morning brought a number
of callers to congratulate them on their
escape, and among them was the man
who had saved their lives. When he entered and found others in the room he
seemed disconcerted and annoyed, but
Miss Mary soon put him more at ease,
for nothing could be more graceful and
charming than the tact and cordiality
with which she made her acknowledg-
ments.

How was it, she asked, that when so few white men were in the theatre he should have been there—just at the right time? And how was it that he had at once thought of the closed door by which escape had become possible?

"Oh," he answered, in a voice that, to their Eastern ears, seemed very Californian or European, for it came from the chest, and the enunciation was different than it often is in the older States, "I have always taken a deep interest in all Old World matters, and the oldest of Old World things can be found among the Chinese; thus I often go to see their plays, and have even learned something of their language. I knew the building intimately, having been there night after night. You probably did not think of this when listening for a time to their somewhat cumbrous play, but it is a fact that, of all spectacles presented to living eyes, a Chinese play is probably the most

unchanged from the earliest times. Of
course, there may have been minor modi-
fications in the art, but essentially the
stage as they have it now is what they
had when Greece and Rome were not,
and we have to go back to Egyptian or
even Assyrian times for anything like it.
Indeed, when the dim dynasties of these
ancient realms were not, China was. The
music you heard at that theatre, the main
features of the representation, were the
earliest growth of civilization."

"Well, certainly, I never thought of
that," said Mary, "except that the funny
man who made the people laugh was
much like an ordinary clown, in the by
play and jokes he was perpetually making."

"Yes, we must have got our clown
from the far East, but I do not think that
he existed on the classic stage of Northern Europe."

"I did not think that you in California

interested yourselves so much in such things," said Mary, in some wonder, as she looked up at the refined and eager face of this man, who seemed an odd mixture of ranchman and reader, "but perhaps you have stayed for some years abroad?"

"Oh, nobody stays very long in San Francisco, for pleasant as the coast is, it becomes monotonous, and one longs after a time for some real winter again," he answered evasively.

"I, too, am very fond of reading, and I hope you will be able to come to see us and talk over our experiences of foreign travel," she replied frankly, "for you are resident here now?"

She could not conceal her curiosity.

"Yes," he answered, "I have come up just in time as it turned out, from some way down the coast, where the old missions of Los Angeles, and Santa Barbara, and Monterey interested me so much that

6

I remained long at those places, which were before unknown to me. If you wish to see the most enchanting portion of this coast you should visit Monterey, where a perpetual sunshine illuminates beautiful woods of sycamore, and, above all, a great grove of cedar, like those of Lebanon. The pines clothe the hillside for some miles, and grow close to the water's edge, so that the breakers of the Pacific fling their spray among the terraced boughs. I wish I could have lived in the days of the old Spanish rule, when first the Christian evangel was brought by the fathers to the Indians who dwelt in numbers on the coast, living on fish and the flesh of the Haleotis shell. They were brave men who first landed in those sunlit bays, and one of them probably in gratitude for safety after some adventure by sea, made his Indians build his church so that the interior of it looks like the inside of a ship, the buttressed ribs curv-

ing from floor to roof. I liked to stand
there in that early church, now ruined,
and to fancy the work of the raising of
God's Temple by the natives with their
feather ornaments on their heads, their
copper-colored skins glowing with the ex-
ertions as they placed the stones or hardened clay bricks, the priest encouraging
them, and near at hand a group of Spanish soldiery with the front and back
curved steel morion on their heads, their
rich doublets, and trunk hose, with pikes
and arquebuses over their shoulders.
For there had been hostile natives to encounter, men who had come from the
great woods in the mountains of the interior, and the Spaniards had experience
enough in the heavy fighting which they
had to face in the South, in Peru and
Mexico, to know that the arm of the flesh
must protect the saints."

He spoke all this with what seemed to
Mary a strange enthusiasm, but it inter-

ested her, and made her still more curious
in regard to the speaker, whose face, figure, and manner, she admired. She liked
to listen to his talk, and was yet struck
with the embarrassment that occasionally
overtook him, as though he feared to betray himself by the very eagerness with
which he pursued a subject that engrossed
his mind for a time. Betray what? That
was the question that arose in her mind.
What was there to conceal? Why for
instance should he suddenly have ceased
to pursue in speech the thoughts that had
once led him after the meetings had become frequent, to talk to her on the
teaching he thought best for a younger
brother of her own, who had just entered
the military academy of the States at
West Point? He had delivered with ardor
a long discourse on the best manner of
preparing a youth to encounter the bat-
tles of life, and then some doubt or hesita-
tion seemed to seize him, and he stopped,

giving some lame apology, obviously not
felt as real by the speaker.

"Ah, but my views on such things can't
interest you, Miss Wincott, and I should
not · have ventured to bore you with
them!"

She felt he knew she was not bored
with them, and yet in one so young as
himself it seemed to her so odd that he
should have cared to think so much
either about missions to ancient heathen
or of the training to be given to boys in
the United States. What on earth could
have made this eccentric young Californian keen on such points? And why again
did he seem not to care to discuss them
with others in whom it might naturally
be expected he would find congenial
companions and controversialists? For
he had on one or two occasions when she
had offered to introduce him to men of
culture and distinction, said he would far
rather talk with her on such things, than

with them. Yet he had not pressed these subjects, for the talk had naturally led to them, and he was quite as much at home and seemed more at ease, although less engrossed with the cause of talk, when conversation fell on horses, sport, botany, or the natural beauties of the wonderful land in which they then found themselves. He had given his name as Chisholm— Walter Chisholm—and was obviously a man of education, and one who had enjoyed opportunities of travel and of life generally, which are not often given to men less wealthy, and that he had made the best of his chances to enrich his mind.

They made an excursion together to the Yosemite Valley to see the " Wellingtonias," as he accidentally called the gigantic Sequoias. " Washingtonias," you mean, she had said, and the incident led to an explanation. They had sat together on the stage, as it swung at a canter round the buffs, where the road has a mountain on one side and a precipice on the other, and she had recounted some of her European adventures of travel to him, and he on his part had shown that the scenes she described were familiar to him.

" Do you know, Mr. Chisholm, I don't believe you are a Californian at all, but an old countryman," she exclaimed, " and you're saying ' Wellingtonia ' in naming our big trees is most outlandish. Now tell me, when did you come to California ?"

" Well, not so very long ago," he answered, and on the following day Mary's father had taken occasion to rally him gravely on his British nomenclature.

" Ah, Mr. Wincott," he said, lightly, " we get back into old habits sometimes, and I have not escaped the failing. Who would have thought it possible that the Britishers would have had the effrontery

to call the biggest plants in America
after Wellington, especially when they
had been appropriated by native bota- .
nists to the glory of the great Virginian?"

"But are you not a Britisher your-
self?" Mr. Wincott said, and Chisholm
replied:

"Since you ask me the question, I am,
although I am not sure that I shall not
settle altogether in some one of these
beautiful valleys, for I like the freedom
of the life, and the scenery is most fascinating. I fear, however, that duties will
call me back to Britain, where my home
used to be, and may have to be again."

He spoke with a certain regret not un-
noticed by the shrewd American, who
had for some time past wished to know
more of the young man to whom they
owed so much, who had now been so
much thrown with his daughter. He suspected that he did not belong to the
"Pacific Slope," and the cast of mind he

had observed in him did not suit the waving locks, and what one of his temporary
companions was pleased to call "that language in his hat." Now that he confessed
himself to be only a sojourner in the
land, although knowing it better than
many who had been born there, he showed
the adaptability of his character by join-
ing in any joke, even though it went
against himself. Thus his enthusiasm for
many things was sometimes a cause of
fun among his new acquaintances, and
in especial his apparent love of authority,
and reverence for those he conceived to
be above him in station was the cause of
much good-humored merriment among
the young Republicans. He was not at
all hurt at their want of comprehension
of his temperament in this respect, and
laughingly told them that he did not believe they would look up even at the big
trees when they were among them, or
acknowledge them to be one whit taller

than the travelers themselves. He used to declare that the subservience shown to dignitaries, whether of the church or state, was not personal service, but the outward form of regard paid to a belief or a cause. One or two of the others professed to admire this, but could not understand it, although, to be sure, the eldest said, " It is the case in the Roman Catholic Church, and I have seen a little feeling expressed in Canada in regard to the monarchy."

" Yes," said Chisholm, with a proud look in his eyes, " there are many who would sacrifice themselves for their faith or their prince."

" Well, for my part, I understand doing anything for a principle, but nothing for a prince."

" I think I could die for my sovereign," said Chisholm, in a low voice, and the other, eying him with a painstaking astonishment, could only reply, slowly :

"Indeed—you don't say so—that must
be an interesting sensation," and added,
with partial assent, "I've known men
ready to die for a dollar, which I take to
be less than a sovereign."

But he became a great favorite with
his new friends, who were only five in
number, nay, her father, a young brother,
and another couple, who had all come
from New England. He had never vol-
unteered to speak to them of himself,
nor had he ever by anything that he had
said assumed any front position, although
his bearing and manner gave the impression that he was a gentleman by birth.
He appeared, indeed, at first too much
occupied with intellectual pursuits to
heed much in what light others regarded
him. It was only after a time, when he
had obviously felt the attraction of
Mary's society, and had yielded to the
magic of her presence, that he had seemed
anxious to conceal that which puzzled

Mr. Wincott, namely, the undoubted aversion he manifested against meeting any
of his own countrymen, that is, any English or Scotch, whom he might happen to
hear were likely to recognize him. This
peculiarity became a source of curiosity
to Mr. Wincott when they returned to
the city, and he could not avoid feeling
some degree of prejudice against the
young man in consequence of it. There
had been so many English adventurers
calling themselves by all the good names
known in England, who had presumed on
the ignorance of Americans, and who had
admitted without question into their society, had, in several cases known to Mr.
Wincott, grossly abused the courtesy and
hospitality accorded to them.

But with Chisholm the case was re-
versed. He had never even mentioned
his own name until pressed to do so, nor
had he seemed at first especially desirous
of making the most of the opportunity

he had to continue an acquaintance begun under circumstances so terrible, and placing his new - found friends under such great obligations to him. Now, indeed, it was different, and he made the most of his time, and was evidently anxious to see as much as he could of Mary. She, on her side, was as evidently interested and charmed by him, and would listen with most unwonted attention and patience while he talked. Another matter which Mr. Wincott had observed was that Mr. Chisholm was exceedingly well lodged, and was therefore evidently a man of some means. He thought, also, that he must be a man of some distinction, for he had let fall observations with regard to men and things that induced his listener to believe that he had seen "many men and cities," in a way not open to those who had not good credentials. It seemed, also, that it was rather in regard to a wish, felt for change of society, than to any other feeling that the avoidance of old countrymen was adopted. Chisholm seemed to be tired of his former life, and to be seeking in the new world variety and difference, rather than any associations with his previous career, whatever that may have been. The exception to this existed in his liking all forms of religious observance, and in his great curiosity in reference to languages and customs. For these things he showed the zeal of a scholar combined with the enthusiasm of a priest. He rather surprised Mr. Wincott by telling him that he, too, wished to go again eastward, and, as he knew that the party he had rescued meant soon to be going homeward, he proposed that they should take steamer to the mouth of the magnificent Columbia River, ascend that stream, and then from some point on Washington State cross over to Vancouver's Island, and finally take the Canadian

Pacific route back to the Atlantic States.
Wincott liked the idea, and the proposal
removed from his mind one last doubt
in regard to his friend, for if there were
anything personally unpleasant to Chisholm in his intercourse with Englishmen
on account of any remembrances of the
past, why should this project be started,
a plan that would inevitably throw him
among many who would recognize and
know all about him if he were a person
who had been known in English society.
Miss Wincott did not give enough credit
to the ignorance of Canadians on such
matters, an ignorance as great as that
prevailing among Americans.   It was,
however, likely that Chisholm might find
quite as many Englishmen likely to know
him in Canada as in Italy, now that the
world-famous railway line of Canada had
attracted so many tourists on account of
the comfort it gave its passengers, and
the wonderful scenery it allowed them to

witness in such perfect comfort and security. Mary took up the idea of an alternative route for their return with enthusiasm. She said she had had quite enough of those horrid alkali plains through which the line from Omaha to 'Frisco had taken them. The brief glimpse of the fine woods after they had crossed the Rockies was but a poor compensation for the dullness of the desert, which the Mormon communities at Ogden and Salt Lake had, to her mind, altogether failed to enliven. They were then all of one purpose, and although a sea-voyage was a thing which was not so acceptable as the rest of the programme, — a fine morning in the early autumn found them embarked on a good steamer, and quitting the golden gates of the wind-vexed harbor of 'Frisco for the mouth of the alp-girdled torrents of the Columbia.

CHAPTER V.

THE vessel leaped into the joyous waters, past the fort-guarded bluffs, and Mary, her young brother, and Chisholm found that for a day or more they would practically have the deck entirely to themselves. The future cadet of West Point, young Wincott, found also that the company of the officers of the ship was quite as lively as was that of his sister and her friend, engaged in conversation which was far too learned for any participation. He didn't a bit mind listening for a time, when Chisholm spoke of his travels, and narrated what he had seen in many strange lands, but when he began to talk at length of what all these good folks believed in the way

7

of religion, and when he sat for a long
time quite silent and only looking at his
sister, who again became, if possible,
more contemplative, and when both
finally not only silently agreed not to
talk, but would not answer him when he
began to hold forth on the most interesting subjects; then, indeed, he thought
that the sooner the rest recovered from
their sea-sickness the more pleasant and
sociable it would be for all concerned.
To do him justice, he did not interrupt
either their silence or their conversation,
the only exception taking place on the
second day of the voyage, when he rushed
aft to tell them of a "splendid sight,"
namely, a whole army of porpoises which
were breaking the water just ahead of
them. Mary went to the side of the vessel, and with her two companions gazed
in astonishment at the curious spectacle.
Almost as far as the eye could reach,
along the slowly heaving waters, a long

line of porpoises appeared, flinging themselves out of the rolling swell, and ad-
vancing northward in an orderly array.
She had seen single individuals, or groups
of a few together follow a ship in the
Atlantic, but here the creatures took no
heed of the steamer, but in their immense
numbers kept an even front for miles
along the ocean, plunging forward as
they follow some mysterious instinct of
migration. The ship soon passed through
them and left them far behind, and now
the voyagers were close to the entrance
of the river, but a strong gale arose, and
made the captain shake his head when he
looked to windward.

" I'll try it anyhow," he said, "for I
have often got over the bar in worse
weather."

Then before the evening had made
navigation more difficult, the vessel
headed in toward the long line of breakers which marked the dreaded bar of the

Columbia. To landsmen the passage of
this place in stormy weather always appears a miracle. Nothing is visible of
the comparatively smooth channel, which
if hit off cleverly gives a safe entrance
among the white tossing waves, whose
angry moan of thunder fills the mind
with terror. The ship seems to be going to certain destruction. The land,
mountainous as it is, appears far off, because the shore is flat for some distance,
and the eye rests only on the white commotion of the surge. The passengers
from San Francisco were all on deck, for
the moment was too interesting and ex-
citing to allow any to remain below, and
from where they stood the waves rose
high above them as they rushed past.
The steamer swayed one way and then
another, rolled and was carried bodily
forward, as the great creamy hillocks
dashed under her, and bore her along.
They were soon in the very thick of the

turmoil, and they gazed at the toppling crests as each hurried on, apparently desirous to choke and fill the watery lane that yawned between it and its immediate predecessor in the awful race for the sand-bar; and they looked amidships where, quietly and calmly the officers and men at the wheel were gathered, watching the conduct of their vessel as they did what they could to guide her. This was most difficult, for the vast hollows made under her stern when a wave had passed, and the next had not yet come, made the propeller revolve with a whirling jar which shook the ship from stem to stern, while the billows that threw her forward with the set of the wind appeared to laugh at the attempts made to direct the toy of wood and iron which they tossed about in derision. There was soon an instant of dreadful suspense, when a heavy shock told them that they had struck the sand, and the momentary

pause on the way of the steamer caused
a wave to fall in hissing masses over the
stern, and to sweep forward in a volume
that would have carried all before it if
the precaution of having everything well
lashed had not been taken. The passengers were behind deck-houses that broke
the force of the water, and saved them
from being swept away. The next moment another mountainous breaker roared
at them, as though to engulf them, but it
lifted the vessel, and she floated free
again, swept on with the speed of wave
and wind.

"Now we are probably safe," said
Chisholm; and so it proved. Each
minute made it apparent that the deeper
channel they had entered lay behind the
ridge of sand which had so nearly wrecked
them. The screw revolved more regu-
larly, catching the surface no more with
only brief snatches; the billows no longer
mounted high alongside and roared them-

selves hoarse as they raced forward. It
was evident that the dire commotion was
being left astern, and that the ship was
not any longer being overtaken by it.
Yes, the bar of the Columbia lay behind
them. The near peril that had threatened their lives so short a while ago, was
over. They hardly realized as yet that
they were saved. But as soon as they
did so, and smooth water was really
reached, an audible " Thank God ! " was
breathed from every lip. It was, indeed,
a signal mercy that had rescued them
from the terrible bar, and in spite of
some mistake as to the exact spot of the
true channel, had carried them unharmed
over a place where many a vessel had
been destroyed. The captain had certainly been foolhardy in attempting the
passage at all, when he might have pro-
ceeded up the coast to the secure entrance to the wide straits of San Juan de
Fuca, and he himself was by no means

anxious to hide the relief he felt, for now that the tension was over, he became talkative and "smokative," if such an expression may be used, and consumed about thirty cigars during the next few hours, burning half and then chewing the remainder of each. The others, in whom we are more immediately interested, were inclined to say very little, but were devoutly thankful that what had seemed imminent death was passed.

Mary and Chisholm went below, for darkness had now come on, and the cheerful lights below were more attractive than the deck, with the monstrous gloom spread around it.

"How strange," said Chisholm, "that in so short a space of time your journey should have brought you into peril by fire and by flood! I fear that you must consider me a man to bring ill luck, for you had no such dangers except when I was present."

"If the luck always turns out so fortunately, I don't think I shall mind your presence much," was the answer, with a quick glance of gratitude. "Have you had any such terrible adventure before?"

"In some ways, perhaps, more trying," said Chisholm, "although as far as actual bodily danger is concerned, I do not think that any one could ever have passed through worse than those of the fire and the threatening shipwreck. But I have felt more tried, and have escaped over an even worse bar than that of the Columbia," he added, with emotion. Mary's curiosity was again aroused, and he continued. "Yes, there are trials of the mind and character, which age men more than these things—would it indeed, interest you to know more of me, Miss Mary? Sometimes I think you doubt me, and I feel that I should like to speak to you as a friend, and know that you have a friendly interest in me. Is it so, and can I hope for some such senti-ment?"

Mary knew by instinct, what might be another peril to her self-possession was close at hand but felt too unnerved to encourage at that moment avowals that she desired secretly to hear, and yet feared because she was aware she would be helpless if he demanded a surrender of her independence. She was not quite prepared to go through more experiences of an agitating nature at that hour, and so she postponed the matter, by asking what could be more dreadful than the storm they had escaped, and saying she only knew of one thing that might be so, and that was, perhaps, the breaking of some affection—the estrangement of some dear friend?

"Yes," he said, to her surprise, "the linking of all ties that bind one to those we love, the rejection of all communion, the bitterness of exile from that we have

most adored and reverenced, the find-
ing that false we have believed to be
true."

"Had he then loved some woman," she
asked herself, "and been rejected? Did
he still," she wondered, "cling to the
memory of one who spurned him? What
could this mean, and if it meant what the
words implied, why was he here, giving
perhaps too much of his regard, winning
much," she almost whispered to herself,
"of her affection?" She said nothing, unless a scarcely audible "yes" indicated
inquiry and regret.

"Yes, I have suffered more than shipwreck in life," he went on, "and the sympathy of a friend is inexpressibly precious
to me. I have touched on a bar in the
great river of life, which has shut me out
from the flow of the mighty river of human kindness."

"Nay," thought Mary, "what an atro-
cious woman it must have been to have

given him so much pain! I should like to see her thrown overboard."

It was quite certain that if Miss Mary had been an autocrat, such as Cleopatra may be supposed to have been when she navigated the Nile in her ancient "Dia Byah," any lady who had offended Walter Chisholm if he had been on board, would have instantly have found himself exploring the bottom of that historic river. This idea made her look rather fierce and intractable. Her admirer, who was himself "getting into deeper water" every moment in speaking to her of his woes, observed the expression, and, being of a very sensitive nature, said:

"But I am a fool to trouble you with my feelings, for what right have I to intrude my insignificant and cheerless talk upon you — especially now when you ought to be having the conversation of some cheerful and amusing companion after the fright you have had to-day?"

"No, pray, Mr. Chisholm, do not say so; but I do not see in what I can help you in mending what the—person—who has vexed you has done. Perhaps you still look to that—person—for restitution of something that has been taken from you. But if you lost your heart," she said, with at attempt at gayety, "it is always a difficult matter, as I am told."

"All lights out please, m'm," at this junction said one of the boat's officials, as a hint that the retirement of the passengers to their cabins was now expected, and further explanations, and disclosures, confidences, and condolences were somewhat abruptly cut short. The morrow was to witness another complication, for at a place where they left the steamer and took to the train they saw on the platform a gentleman who scrutinized Chisholm with much attention, and was soon occupied in earnest conversation with a companion, who also looked in

the same direction, when both, with a
gesture of aversion, entered another car.
Chisholm had seen these two men also,
and turned his back upon them, as he
helped Miss Mary and her father into
the other car. A reference to his acquaintances on the platform soon came
from Miss Mary, who perceived that the
gentlemen she had observed looking at
them and speaking eagerly were known
to him.

"Oh, yes, they are known to me, but I
do not think they will care to speak to
me," he answered, somewhat sadly.

"I suppose they are reporters for some
of the newspapers," she remarked, a little maliciously, "for it is evident that
they take much interest in your move-
ments."

"Ah," he said, with a forced smile,
"perhaps it was you, Miss Mary, who
engaged their attention and any admiration their looks may have conveyed, was,

I am certain, not excited by my appearance."

It was evident that he did not care to pursue this subject, and no further allusion was made to it. But their journey was to carry them past the flourishing American cities now rising on the United States coast, and they took ship again to cross over to Vancouver's Island, where they designed to pass a few days at Victoria, there to rest awhile before again undertaking the transcontinental journey. It was while crossing over the straits, and while Wincott was admiring the splendid view of the Olympian Range that walled to the south the calm waters, that he was accosted by one of the men who had watched so closely himself and Chisholm as they took the cars a day or two before. The stranger began by lifting his hat and making some ordinary observations about the scenery and the weather. He was well clad in a dark

suit of clothes, with a hat having a sug-
gestion in "its language" of clericalism,
an idea further strengthened by the cut
of his collar, which also "spoke" of a
subtle eloquence having occasionally
been delivered from under its narrow but
immaculate and close-fitting edge. His
address was good, and the accents decidedly British.   Mr. Wincott was naturally
polite, but, unlike some Americans, he
had almost a British antipathy to being
interrupted in his thoughts by any un-
looked-for intrusion. He therefore answered somewhat briefly, and did not
offer to continue the conversation. But
the darkly-clad gentleman soon again, in
the gentlest of voices, expressed the
pleasure it gave him (for he was, he said,
an Englishman) to find that an eminent
citizen of the Eastern States intended to
visit an English colony such as Vancouver, and said that he had been there
long enough to know the value of inter-

national good understanding, a result
that could best be arrived at by mutual
knowledge, and how could such knowledge be better obtained than by the personal visits of influential men on both
sides!

Mr. Wincott did not care for this
style of flattery, and merely bowed. His
coldness was remarked by his agreeable
besieger, and the attack was changed,
and the tone altered to one calculated to
awake a more responsive spirit.

"I hope I may be permitted to present
to your daughter a brief account of the
history of this part of the world. I have
seen how she admires the country, and
its natural history has only been touched
by poor Lord's pen, while there is much
that would interest her in its early dis-
covery from the time of the Dutch Vancouver to the days commemorated by
Washington Irving in 'Astoria.'"

"I thank you, sir," replied Wincott.

8

"I presume I have the pleasure of addressing a resident of the West Coast."

"No, I have but lately come here, but, as I have had a good training, that makes me a good hand at learning languages. I have been much among the Indians, and have taken a deep interest in them, and my work has laid chiefly among them and the Chinese. I should like to be of service to you, and perhaps you will not take it amiss if I ask one question of you, for you have among your party one I know well. May I inquire if my old acquaintance Chisholm has been long with you."

"No, sir; but, if you know him, how is it that you do not put the question to him, instead of to me?"

"It is because I have a special reason for the inquiry, and if he is not a friend of yours, and you have but known him recently, I can do so."

"Sir, he is, I believe, a countryman of

your own, but I have not been so curious
about him as you appear to be, and I
have not questioned him."

"Perhaps it is as well that you did
not," was the reply, "for I fear you
would not get the truth from him."

Wincott looked at his questioner in
great surprise.

"Sir, I do not think we need discuss
such matters."

"It is because I wished to give you a
solemn warning against him that I have
ventured to say so much," replied the
man, with imperturbable suavity, as
though he was saying the pleasantest
thing in the world. "I have known
Walter Chisholm, for such is his name,
for some years, and believe me that he
is here for no good. He has betrayed
those who trusted him in Europe, and he
will betray again any man or woman who
confides in him."

"Sir, you have said enough," was Wincott's answer, and he bowed to the communicative gentleman a low bow, that clearly indicated an end to the conversation.

Such confidences, however, do not leave an agreeable impression behind them, and Wincott found himself eying with increased attention, and with an easiness he could not control, the good understanding that had evidently sprung up between Mary and Walter. He went so far as to take occasion to say a word to his daughter, in the nature of a reminder that people were not always to be at once implicitly to be trusted, however great an obligation might be owing to them, and urged that a long acquaintance should always precede the forming of any irretrievable decisions. Mary listened patiently, but only said when he concluded:

"Papa, is it not true that these men who came on board with us have been speaking to you of Mr. Chisholm?"

Wincott had eluded giving any positive reply, which, of course, made Mary certain that the fact was as she and Chisholm had surmised.

"But why, then, does he not," she thought, as she meditated on this, "why does not Mr. Chisholm challenge these eavesdroppers and slanderers?"

Before long they arrived at Victoria, and pushed their way along the quay, which was crowded with people who had come down to meet the boat. There were many Chinese—indeed, most of the men there wore the pig-tail and blue loose tunic of that nationality. But there were many whites, who directed the operations of the yellow men in clearing the boat. There were a few Tartar-faced Indians—"ugly creatures," as Mary thought—with big cheek bones, and eyes set at an angle only a little less than the Chinese. There were also ruddy Englishmen, who heartily greeted the passengers they expected to meet. Among these was a man of good countenance, who, as soon as he saw Chisholm, shouted out:

"Hullo, Walter, old fellow, what on earth brings you here? By Jove, I am glad to see you! Come to turn over a new leaf altogether in the new world, eh? Are you alone? Come to my house. Goodness gracious, what a surprise to see you, old man, and what a pleasure!" and then ran on in the same strain, asking so many questions that it was impossible to answer them. Chisholm's face glowed with delight at the meeting with his friend, and Mary shared in his joy, on seeing him so warmly welcomed.

"No, I am not alone, in one sense, for I have been in the company of these friends," said Chisholm. "Let me introduce you to them," and then he made known his name as the Honorable Charles Churston, an old English public school-

mate of his own. Nothing would satisfy
Churston until Chisholm had promised to
go to his house instead of going to the
Russell House Hotel, where they had all
ordered rooms.

"Will you follow on after you have got
the luggage," said Churston, "and, in the
mean time, if Mr. Wincott allows me, I
will show himself and Miss Wincott the
way to the hotel, and see they get all
they need." He made them mount a
nicely appointed buggy, and, as he drove
them away, said to Mr. Wincott:

"Well, I consider myself to be in great
luck to have met you, especially with
such a dear old friend as Chisholm—the
best fellow I know."

Wincott told him that he esteemed Mr.
Chisholm, and that he had saved them
from a great danger at San Francisco.

"Well, I am glad to hear he has fallen
in with you, for I am sure he could not
be in better hands. I have good reason

to respect and love him, and no man in my estimation has shown a finer character than his—and well tried it has been, too," he added in a lower tone.

They drove on through the clean and bright streets of the delightful capital of the great Province of British Columbia. There was plenty of life in the highways and by-ways. Cheerful buildings of red brick bespoke a comfort unalloyed by extravagant attempts at display, good shops with ample fronts of glass were sheltered from the sun by the verandaed sidewalks, which the travelers had noticed in use in the big city that they had left a few days before. From many points the joyous waters of the bay and of the calm straits could be seen, the shadowy mountains on the farther American continent shining with the dim snows upon their summits. Hills on the island around them rose green with the forests of the handsóme Douglas fir. Over all breathed an air of peaceful prosperity, not achieved without effort, but maintained without the fever manifest in more ambitious places. A perfect climate, a contented people, a free and happy life, occupied but not distracted by its daily business, these seemed the characteristics of a country whose motto might be given in the words "Loyal and Laborious." By loyalty and labor they had won a position to be envied. They had enough for their wants; there were none very rich to make them envious. There were only enough poor to remind them of the virtue of charity. Their land was beautiful and their lives were happy.

CHAPTER VI.

It may readily be imagined that Mary Wincott had by this time made a confidante of the only other lady of her party, and this lady took a most lively interest in all she heard, fully sympathized with Mary in her admiration for Chisholm, and was ready, as most good women are, to clear up any misunderstandings and difficulties which might have prevented a marriage.

"You may think how badly I felt," said Mary, "when my father spoke to me on the subject of Mr. Chisholm's attentions. He seemed to think that those bilious-looking men on the steamer, had truth on their side when they spoke against my friend. I consider them both as frauds, and although they should be intelligent, judging from the number of bumps and lumps on their heads, I think Mr. Chisholm's calm fair brow is decidedly worth a thousand such mean intellects."

This was pretty strongly expressed, but Miss Wincott's mind had been much exercised on the subject; and where the heart feels the mouth speaks. Her anxiety was heightened next morning when her friend did not appear, and when a letter was handed to her father, which she could see bore Mr. Chisholm's handwriting on the cover. We may as well give the contents of this letter. What it conveyed could hardly influence the young lady's mind for or against the writer, because her opinions were already so firmly established that it is safe to say that nothing short of a miracle would have changed them. Her father had been most favorably impressed by all he had heard from Mr. Churston, but he had not cleared up any doubts that might arise in consequence of the peculiarities he had noticed in Chisholm—the dislike of meeting those he might have been supposed to be likely to be willing to meet, and the somewhat mysterious references he had to let fall as to the vexations of his past life. Mr. Wincott said nothing when he received the letter, but retired to his room. Thither we may follow him, and read the letter over his shoulder.

CHAPTER VII.

Letter from Mr. Chisholm to Mr. Wincott.

"DEAR SIR: I hope you will not be angry with me if I ask your kind attention to a very long letter. I might, perhaps, not have addressed it to you, had I not heard before we left San Francisco, that family circumstances, which would have deterred me from writing it, had been changed by a judicial decision given on a pending suit in the Scottish Courts. This decision leaves me the master of a fortune that renders me quite independent. Owing to events which I shall take the liberty of explaining to you, this matter rested in doubt for some time.

" I have been assured by your considerate conduct toward me, that events

which concern me may not be wholly in-
different to you. If they be of no interest to you, I do not request you to pro-
ceed in the perusal of this communication.
I feel, however, that unless I make you
the offer of an explanation, I may remain
in a false position, and I have had too
evil an experience of a false position to
allow me not to make the attempt, at all
events, to save myself from again becoming the victim of another such misfortune.
The death of my father occurred a few
months ago, and it has added to the distress I have felt on other accounts that I
was not able to receive his blessing on his
deathbed, nor to remove from his mind
prejudices which he had conceived against
me. These prejudices were founded on
conduct on my part of which you your-
self shall be the judge, if you read this
letter to the end. Suffice it to say now,
that they were sufficiently strong to prevent his contributing in any form to my

support when I had occasion to apply to him.

"He told me when I was still quite young, and had taken the first step that led to his displeasure, that if I persisted in the course I had felt it my duty to take, he could not give me the aid he had given to others of his family. As I was the eldest, and had a natural right to expect favor at his hands, this announcement did not tend to soften my feelings, but rather hardened me to shape an independent course, believing that injustice had followed misrepresentation. That my path was not his, that my opinion led me on a different way, was, I knew, a grief to him, but I did not expect that he would have taken the side of my enemies.

"My persistence soon led to his sending to me an intimation that he had disinherited me. But this also had no effect on me. Indeed, from the manner of life I had chosen to lead when this new meas-

ure of his displeasure fell upon me, I had
expected little else. I was not surprised,
although I was pained by the manner in
which the decision was conveyed to me,
and by the additional words of reproof
with which it was accompanied. I could,
however, not have used the property, as I
then conceived, for my own good, and regretted its loss only because I fancied that
therewith I might have done good to
others. Now since his death all is changed.
It was found by my legal representatives
that the old Scots entail through which in
his phrase he could 'drive a coach and
six,' still held good. The wish of my
parent to devise the land otherwise than
it has been devised from father to son
through a very long array of ancestors is
therefore rendered a nugatory and I am
in possession of that he owned. Although
by no means a rich heritage, it is far more
than sufficient. I have been accustomed
to live as though I should literally have

to take no care for the morrow as to what
I should eat or what I should drink. I
find myself still wondering whether it is
right to spend what is mine, still waking
with surprise to find that I am to wear
good clothes, still inclined to grudge myself that which all those of my station in
life enjoy without thought, and use without examination or gratitude. The old
poverty and faith that made me not care
for the morrow, is replaced by a consciousness that what has become mine without
labor should be shared by those who can
hardly attain by any effort the comfort I
have. The vow of charity I hold to be
a holier vow than that of poverty. The
acceptance of the will of Providence in
bestowing that which is good is best
shown by the filling of the burden of the
responsibility of its distribution. We
should not, I believe, fly from this pen-
ance of life, and leave to others that which
we should do ourselves. To hide our in-

9

dividuality for an association of mortals
like ourselves, and to vow obedience to
one of these in matters in which the giving of that which is ours, not as seems
best to the intellect planted in ourselves,
but as seems best only to a fellow-man
chosen as our superior, seems to me a
sacrifice to man rather than to God. I
have interpreted the phrase used by my
former friends of the abdication of the
empire over self-will, and have found it to
mean the enthronement of a will more to
be distrusted than our own.

"Let each man use the intellect given
to him; let no man surrender it to others
in the lesson I have learned. I have not
found peace in the suppression of my own
thoughts, nor have I found rest in forsak-
ing the place appointed me by Providence
in the line of life's battle. You will wonder at this apparently irrelevant rhap-
sody, but the explanation is briefly this—
my father disapproved of my becoming a

Roman Catholic, and of the further steps taken by me in that most holy faith. It was the after consequences of my action that he detested, with the unreasoning dislike of a man who has never had the patience to look into questions, even though he had heard them superficially criticised. It was not so much my reception into that Church that he dreaded, but the acceptance by me of priests' orders, which I was privileged to bear some time afterward. He declared that a priest must give all he had to the church, and that as I could have no family or affection outside of its pale, he must pass me over, and give my inheritance to another. I am no priest now; I have left the communion I embraced. I am a double-dyed traitor in the eyes both of my family and my old brethren of the priesthood. Can you wonder that I feel a terror of meeting those who believe me forsworn? Can you not at this same time understand how it is that I entered that church in my youth for conscience' sake, embraced the religion by which I was attracted, and have also done right in returning to that in which I was christened, when the priestly vocation did not satisfy me and when my conscience no longer allowed me to wear the uniform denoting obedience to its officers, and belief in its trusts? Thus much I say at the outset, that you may not misunderstand me, for I can not bear that I should long delay in placing before you my reason for the doubt you must have seen in my bearing, and that I should not at once declare that I am not ashamed of what I have done, however much I may shrink from the constant assertion of my integrity before those who would dispute it.

"But I have not told you all. More must yet be said. Let me ask your patience.

"I was an impressionable youth, and

had from a very early age liked to pore
over books, containing what I may call
the heraldry of religion, for the forms of
the churches are but the blazon of belief.
The pageantry that is always attractive
to the wondering child-nature within us, a
nature that is impressed by ceremonies
and costumes, and scenic effect, especially
if they be made to have mysterious mean-
ings; the love of beauty in music, in
lights, in colors, which the boy or girl
shares in common with the elder child,
the savage, or the uneducated—all this
had a double fascination for me. But as
a youth I was by no means untouched by
the simple forms of worship. I used to
attend the services of the Orthodox or
Greek Church, and loved to listen to the
deep-toned chanting of their priests, and
delighted in the mysterious secrecy of the
painted screen, rich with the hues of all
metals and jewelry surrounding the figures of the saints. My curiosity in eccle-

siastical matters went so far that I sat
observing with the greatest attention not
only the services but even the debates in
the assemblies of Protestant churches.
Perhaps it was the constant strain on the
mind, caused by watching how much all
these doctors differed in the prescriptions
they offered for its weal, that aggravated
a temperament which in youth was too
sensitive, as is the case with many boys.
The delicacy of constitution which marked
my early years gave way with manhood,
but the doubts and questionings of heart
and soul that a more healthy tone would
have preserved me from, left its impress
upon me. I became, when still a child,
what the French call a *dévot*. I believed
that I could assist in the regeneration of
mankind. Among my studies had, of
course, been the writings of the Fathers
of the Catholic Church, and I had taken
opportunities of conversing upon these
with members of that church. An excel-

lent man, who belonged to that faith, soon saw the aptitude I possessed for instruction and took me in hand with a zeal worthy of a better cause. He was desirous not only to secure me, but the property that he believed would be mine, and, without telling any of my family, I was admitted by him to the church. I do not blame him, for I know that he acted as he thought for my good. It was some time before the truth of my conversion was known to my father, and his anger made me, as I say, a yet firmer adherent of the doctrines I had embraced. I conceived myself to be already in some measure a martyr, and that the punishment I suffered in this world would be more than rewarded in the next. But my health was none the better for the anxiety I endured, and the weaker I became in body the more was I shut out by my new pastors from any influences but their own. Soon my highest ambition was the priesthood.

"I begged to be allowed to study at Rome. Then from exposure to the sun, and the consequence of a cold caught when sleeping in a little room hidden away from the light, and therefore damp and chilly, I fell very ill. Again, in spite of all the kindness of those who ministered to me, a renewed state of uncertainty as to my future, a dependent frame of mind took possession of me and tortured me with misgivings, and doubts, so that I often even longed for death. The reminiscences of childhood, the desire again to experience the love of my kindred, were mingled with intensely vivid pictures of the place I loved in my youth; the woods, and hills, and glens, and streams, along which my way used to take me.

"In my ravings I panted for the cool rush of the Highland burns, the soothing babble of the quieter reaches in the meadows so full of primroses in the spring, and starred even in the autumn with the ox-eye daisies. I raved against all that had induced me to leave such happiness, the joys shared with parents and brothers and sisters at home. It was raving, I suppose, for I had been told that I had been delirious, and surely such weaknesses were wholly unworthy of one who had put his hand to the plow and durst not turn back.

"Certainly as I grew stronger the fearful homesickness and yearning for the old days and the old ways, left me to a great extent, and I looked forward again to fulfilling my vows as a soldier of Christ. It was when I was recovering that I read the lives of the saints, and the fortune and career of the founder of the Jesuit fraternity, deeply interested me. I could not help in some measure comparing his fate with my own, for he also had been born to competence, and a position honorable in his own country.

He had had greater fortune than I, for he had distinguished himself in battle, and when wounded had first turned his thoughts to piety and God. It was a fanciful and conceited thought on my part, to think of my own case in connection with his glorious success and marvelous self-confidence. But I was still weak, and conceit is one of the courtiers of a feeble brain. An ambition was at all events aroused to do what he had done, to make his knightly breeding and bearing the stepping-stone to a place wherein to wield authority greater than that even of the most successful warrior. My studies were renewed, and in the intervals of my work I wandered to some massive ruin of Pagan times, in Rome, and felt how great the creed must be that vanquished the building of these leviathan baths, and theatres, and temples, and palaces, and felt how the spirit of Peter and of Paul had lived again in such men

as Loyola, although in different guise,
and perhaps sullied with more natural
aspiration. The soldier and cavalier had
not the advantage which the fishermen
possessed, of following so close upon the
Master. He had not been able to see
Him, and hear from His lips the words
that made death seem as nothing, and
even pain if it must come, welcome as a
seal of their covenant with Him, and an
ensign for the guidance of all men in the
ways they had walked with Him. But
although the type of the conquering
spirit was wholly different, yet the Span-
iard and the Galileans had both fought
the good fight, and if mistakes had been
committed by the successors of Loyola,
had not equally grievous mistakes been
committed by the successors of St. Peter?

"I used to go to the churches when
worn out with pacing the streets and
country, and would sit down or kneel
before some altar, heart and limb wearied,

and feeling the coolness and the darkness
of the place more soothing than I can
express. On one of these days I had
felt disturbed by some chanting which
had broken forth in the chancel, and had
wandered forth again, only to enter beneath another great front, whose doors
were receiving many persons. It was
near evening. The church was great and
solemn in the gloom, but there was nothing visible in it which especially distinguished it from many another beautiful
edifice. The lofty roof, the round arches
which divided the chapels in the aisles
from the nave, the semicircular vault
above the high altar, were like those of
other places of Roman worship. They,
too, were built as were the old temples
with that perfect curve of round vaulting
which was bequeathed to their descend-
ants by the masters of the ancient world.
But it was too dark to criticise the archi-
tecture or to be conscious of more than

the vastness or solemnity of this Christian temple. Wandering on into the church, with a vague desire to kneel nearer to the great altar, upon which were numerous lights burning like the shore of a harbor of refuge seen across a waste of black waters, I found several worshipers there before me, and turned into the transept and kneeled before a marble balustrade which guarded a shrine on which were set no candles. I completed my prayer and rose, and then saw that apparently coming from the steps before me shone a glow of light, which made the inner part of the shrine bright with the sheen of gold. This upward gleaming of light from the steps before me led me to gaze more nearly at it, and I saw on the worked metal the figure of a man who was giving an open volume to others who pressed around him to receive it. The dress of this figure was unmistakable. It was the Jesuit dress, and this was the figure of Loyola, and I was standing at his tomb. I was profoundly impressed with the circumstance that had led me to this sepulchre, for I knew not, so short had been my sojourn in Rome while in health, where the Church of the Jesu stood. I had entered it unwittingly, I had been conducted, as I thought, by an unseen but directly guiding power to this holy place, the grave of one of whom I had lately read so much, and with whose spirit I had felt a sympathy that had drawn mine to his. And now, on a platform near the pulpit, I saw a Jesuit priest ascend in order to address the crowd who were filling the center part of the building. He waited until most of them had seated themselves, and I saw his dark robes and dark square cap becoming gradually less and less distinct in the dusk. There was a little lamp hanging from the center of the arch which vaulted each aisle

chapel, and near one of these he stood,
and then began to preach in a voice so
full of earnestness, so silently, with an
intense consciousness of the transcend-
ent importance and the truth of the mes-
sage .he was commissioned to give, that
I listened spell-bound. His white face
could be seen moving a little from side
to side, his arms as they were raised
lifted the long sleeves that rose and fell
at his sides like black wings. The people were very silent, and bent forward
to hear, as his full voice boldly explained
his dogma, and then pleads with them
most touchingly to hear and to follow
where the saintly founder of their society, the servant of God, had led. He
did not plead in vain with me. I became
not only a priest, but also a Jesuit.

"The severe discipline to which all
those who desire to enlist in the Company of Jesus are subjected fell heavily
upon me, and when at last I was admitted

to exercise my new functions I was an
austere ascetic. Some disappointment
and chagrin was, I am ashamed to say,
allowed to rankle in my breast, for an
eager novice naturally expects to be received with open arms, when once he has
given up his whole life, and desires to
embrace the new duty. He is apt to believe that the severity of the wrench his
own feelings have undergone, should be
the measure of the warmth of the greet-
ing accorded to him when he enters the
new fold. When on the contrary, except
for the congratulations of his own inti-
mates, he finds the order he joins is, at
all events as far as regards its official or
public conduct toward him, apparently
suspicious and distrustful, he resents the
coldness of his reception. He thinks he
has already in all he has suffered proved
his sincerity, and that further tests are
unnecessary—a worry—nay, almost an
insult. The meekness and obedience he

should feel have not yet fully entered
into the fiber of his thought, and he is
inclined to think that his sacrifice has
not been accepted, and that he is worthy
of greater trust. He knows that it is
useless to ask for responsibility where
the authority to which he has yielded,
has not yet decreed that such shall be
given to him. He undergoes his discipline, but he often repines. It was so
with me, and my tendencies were not un-
discovered, nor was it thought good that
I should be tried beyond what I could
bear. It is not the policy of the society
to do anything to a man which might
lose him to its cause, or even render his
enthusiasm less fervent. It was desired
that I should be retained among them
and employed to win others over. Each
of my utterances had been repeated, and
although I was not in the habit of saying
much, yet all that had escaped me together with the evidence of the moods

that had possessed me, was sufficient for
the superiors of the Order to deem that
my health was to be strengthened, my
mind braced, and a very generous course
of treatment accorded to me, so that I
might again take my place among men,
and work for the greater glory of God in
the world. I was to be an instructor of
youths, and boys do not like a severe
ascetic as their playmate and companion.
My director therefore encouraged me to
eat good food, and lead my life as much as
possible in the open air, and to live much
as I would have lived had I remained in
the house of a country gentleman. This
ultimately restored to me my former
strength, and was perhaps also the cause
of my future release from the bonds and
meshes they had cast and woven around
me. For a long while I worked diligent-
ly, I endeavored to the very best of my
power to subdue any rebellious thoughts
that arose in me. My own inclinations

had always pointed to missionary work, and I had conceived a great desire to have China allotted as the field of my labors. But I was told such was not my destination, and that I could be of more use at home. During the time I remained under instruction there was much in the teaching I received that was repulsive to me, and was, I thought, against the spirit of the Founder of the Order, for whose pure and gallant life I retained the greatest veneration. How could I, for instance, agree that the maxim of one of their most renowned writers was consistent with truth, when he wrote: 'If a man commit a crime, reflecting indeed, but still very imperfectly and superficially, upon the wickedness and great willfulness of those crimes, however heinous may be the matter, he still sins but lightly. The reason is that as a knowledge of the wickedness is necessary to constitute the sin, so it is a full clear knowledge and

reflection necessary to constitute a heinous sin. And thus, as Vasquez says, in
order that a man may freely sin, it is
necessary to deliberate whether he sins
or not. But he fails to deliberate upon
the moral wickedness of it, if he does not
reflect, at least by doubting upon it, during the act. Therefore he does not sin
until he reflects upon the wickedness of
it. It is certain that a full knowledge is
requisite to constitute mortal sin.'

"Was not this maxim, and others like
it, which I still found in favor, worthily
denounced by that pope who was un-
doubtedly poisoned by the Jesuits because he suppressed their order in Rome?
What said this pope—Ganganelli—as late
as the last century: 'Further concerning
the use of certain maxims which the Holy
See has with reason prescribed as scanda-
lous and manifestly contrary to good
morals.' Yet it was by these lights that
I was commanded to walk, for in course

of time I became under this recommen-
dation tutor to the heir of another family,
situated somewhat like my own, that is
having a good estate, which was to de-
volve upon the boy placed under my instruction. I was here gradually pressed
more and more by my immediate superior
to do things against which my whole soul
revolted. I do not blame the general of
the order or the higher authorities, for I
believe that they were misled by false re-
ports coming from the priest whose orders
I was obliged more immediately to obey.
But I perceived after a time that this man
had persuaded himself that it would be
within the bounds of possibility for his
conscience to prevent the lad from marry-
ing, and knowing that he would have absolute control over the lad and goods, for
the boy had been born after the date of
the act which forbade the entail of land
on children born after its passage through
Parliament. He would therefore be free

to do what he chose with the property,
and if he did not marry, might dispose of
it 'to the greater glory of God.' It may
be that I wronged my superior in fancy-
ing that to be his object. Whether this
be so or not I suspected that it was, and
wrote to him a violent letter, for my in-
dignation was aroused by the base suspicion—a suspicion I must own—which
was based on very slight grounds. The
idea was indignantly disowned and a report sent against me to headquarters.

"My old headstrong impulse had returned to me with my recovery of health,
and I swore aloud that I would no longer
submit. The very terms to the reply of
my letter, the subtle lies as I thought
them to be, impressed on each page made
my passion greater. I wrote again saying
that I should never wear again 'the livery
of my moral disgrace,' as I called my
clerical dress. Without a word to the
family with whom I was living I left, and

changing my name resided for some time in a town where I could not be easily tracked, even if any one had cared to take the trouble to follow me, which was by no means likely. After I had left, a reaction set in, and I half regretted my passion and the course it had led me to take.

"Loneliness is bad for man, and solitariness in a great city makes loneliness feel doubly miserable. I could not approach my family. They had given me up as a blacksheep long ago, and did not wish to rearrange the partition they fancied they could make of our estate. I could not venture near any of the brethren I had left, for I should be received by them either too kindly as willing to return, or not at all, and treated as a renegade and traitor. Shame seemed to darken round me on every side, and yet gradually I knew that I had on the whole been right in what I had done, although I may have done what

was right too passionately and too im-
pulsively. A longing came over me to
see again the country of my birth and
boyhood. I found friends among the
tenants of the estate, and lived among
them for a month. Then I escaped from
my own thoughts, and from the idleness
that made them get more bitter, and took
passage for America. There, after a
year, I had the happiness of meeting you
and your daughter, in the Chinese theatre.
Should you condemn me, I shall ask you
not to let your daughter see this letter.
Should you, on the whole, approve of my
conduct, I request you to allow her to
read it, for her good opinion has become
to me that which I most value and regard
in life."

Mr. Wincott was not a man to deliberate too long on any question. His
opinion was gradually formed and reso-
lutely adhered to, and the opinion he had

on the case laid before him in the letter
was accurately expressed when he closed
its perusal and said:

"Quite right. Better late than never.
He might have imagined the set of that
current before he embarked on it. I'll
give Mary the letter."

That young lady also retired to her
room to read it, and her prevalent feeling
was expressed when she concluded in the
words—"What a horrid shame!"—by
which she doubtless meant that Chisholm
had been all along in the right, and
everybody he had disagreed with had
been in the wrong. He came to receive
his sentence next morning, and was
unanimously acquitted by the judge and
jury. He certainly would never have
feared another earthly tribunal so much
as he did that of the Wincott party,
and I doubt if even the General of the
Jesuits could have infused into him a
tithe of the fear that secretly possessed

him as he approached the door. To judge from his face, when he left the door, the grand inquisition within had not put him to the torture. He walked quite straight, and was firm on his legs. A smile on his lips and a light in his eyes spoke of what his former friends would have pronounced, in their language—"justification and peace." Not many days elapsed before he had declared that he could not face the criticism of the East unless he had Mary to exorcise any evil spirits that might linger around him or meet him in the world he had left, and she had vowed to defend him against devil or saint.

"Who would have thought that I should meet my fate in 'Frisco," she laughingly said, "and at the hands of a man, too, who had never seen me in polite society, and appeared for the first time like a Chinese dragon to carry me off in the midst of flames and smoke?"

"Ah, but I saw you in polite society long before our 'Frisco meeting," he said.

"No—how was that? Where?" was the natural inquiry.

"Don't you remember a certain visit paid by you to a smuggler's cave in Scotland?" he asked.

"Why, yes; you don't mean to say that you were the ghost we saw in the cave?"

"Yes; I had been staying in the farmhouse, you remember, near the cave, and had asked the good people to keep quiet about my return for a time to my old haunts, and was reading one day in that cavern, which I dearly loved to visit, when you and your party entered, and I had an opportunity to see you sitting, and eating, and talking, and never forgot you from that moment."

"No, impossible; there was only an old man, who disappeared—an old man with a white beard."

He laughed and said:

"What, my poor old book, the volume I had with me? There was no white beard, but the book I held near my face may have seemed like one in the dark, and the ledge to which I ascended was hidden from your candles, so that you never saw me, but I saw you well. I was at one moment almost tempted to join you, but my foolish fear of being again seen by people who might talk about me, and tell many who would recognize me, prevented me. Besides, I am not sorry, for I was perhaps able to make a better impression at the theatre than I could have hoped to do even in that romantic place."

"Well, I consider you took a base advantage of us," said Miss Mary, "but you must have been known to that farmer and his neighbors."

"Yes, but they kept my secret in all my trouble. I never disguised myself, nor did I ever change my name."

"Then you have behaved better than I, for I have promised you to change my name," said Mary.

And she has kept her promise, and now speaks with a very British accent, and has a property that she and her husband sometimes call the Smuggler's Cave. To this the reader may some day be invited, and if he makes the expedition he will see the ghost, and Mary Chisholm, who has never since the day we quoted her as using the expression ever again said "that she felt badly."

THE END.

*T*HE GARDEN'S STORY; or, Pleasures and Trials of an Amateur Gardener. By GEORGE H. ELLWANGER. With Head and Tail Pieces by Rhead. 12mo. Cloth extra, $1.50.

"Mr. Ellwanger's instinct rarely errs in matters of taste. He writes out of the fullness of experimental knowledge, but his knowledge differs from that of many a trained cultivator in that his skill in garden practice is guided by a refined æsthetic sensibility, and his appreciation of what is beautiful in nature is healthy, hearty, and catholic. His record of the garden year, as we have said, begins with the earliest violet, and it follows the season through until the witch-hazel is blossoming on the border of the wintry woods. . . . This little book can not fail to give pleasure to all who take a genuine interest in rural life. They will sympathize with most of the author's robust and positive judgments, and with his strong aversions as well as his tender attachments."—*Tribune,* New York.

*T*HE FOLK-LORE OF PLANTS. By T. F. THIS-ELTON DYER, M. A. 12mo. Cloth, $1.50.

"The Folk-Lore of Plants" traces the superstitions and fancies connected with plants in fairy-lore, in witchcraft and demonology, in religion, in charms, in medicine, in plant language, etc. The author is an eminent English botanist, and superintendent of the gardens at Kew.

"A handsome and deeply interesting volume. . . . In all respects the book is excellent. Its arrangement is simple and intelligible, its style bright and alluring; authorities are cited at the foot of the page, and a full index is appended. . . . To all who seek an introduction to one of the most attractive branches of folk-lore, this delightful volume may be warmly commended."—*Notes and Queries.*

*F*LOWERS AND THEIR PEDIGREES. By GRANT ALLEN, author of "Vignettes of Nature," etc. Illustrated. 12mo. Cloth, $1.50.

No writer treats scientific subjects with so much ease and charm of style as Mr. Grant Allen. His sketches in the magazines have well been called fascinating, and the present volume, being a collection of various papers, will fully sustain his reputation as an eminently entertaining and suggestive writer.

"'Flowers and their Pedigrees,' by Grant Allen, with many illustrations, is not merely a description of British wild flowers, but a discussion of why they are, what they are, and how they come to be so; in other words, a scientific study of the migration and transformation of plants, illustrated by the daisy, the strawberry, the cleavers, wheat, the mountain tulip, the cuckoo-pint, and a few others. The study is a delightful one, and the book is fascinating to any one who has either love for flowers or curiosity about them."—*Hartford Courant.*